Standing

Ernest McMillan

Standing

ONE MAN'S ODYSSEY THROUGH
THE TURBULENT '60S

LA REUNION PUBLISHING

DALLAS, TEXAS

La Reunion Publishing, an imprint of Deep Vellum
3000 Commerce St., Dallas, Texas 75226

Deep Vellum is a 501c3 nonprofit literary arts organization founded in 2013 with the mission to
bring the world into conversation through literature.
deepvellum.org · @deepvellum

Deep Vellum is a 501c3 nonprofit literary arts organization
founded in 2013 with the mission to bring
the world into conversation through literature

First US Edition, 2023

LIBRARY OF CONGRESS CATALOGING-IN-PUBLICATION CONTROL NUMBER: 2023934937

ISBN (TPB) 978-1-64605-209-7
ISBN (Ebook) 978-1-64605-235-6

Cover image: Danny Lyon

Cover design by Zoe Guttenplan | zoeguttenplan.com

Interior layout and typesetting by KGT

PRINTED IN THE UNITED STATES OF AMERICA

*To those invincible, unseen guides: Spirit, Heart, Ancestors, Angels,
Orishas, who often whisper with oh so soft, gentle nudges, and then, when
absolutely required, heavy, blistering jolts . . .*

To my offspring:

*Angela Lanette, Ernest Ohene Kitiwa, and Dafina Toussainte
And through their respective journeys
May you forever be a light unto yourself*

CONTENTS

PART ONE: THE CALLING

Chapter One   3
Chapter Two   9
Chapter Three   19
Chapter Four   29

PART TWO: MOVEMENT

Chapter Five   37
Chapter Six   49
Chapter Seven   56
Chapter Eight   62

PART THREE: ON THE RUN

Chapter Nine   81
Chapter Ten   96
Chapter Eleven   106
Chapter Twelve   114
Chapter Thirteen   120
Chapter Fourteen   125

PART FOUR: PRISON LETTERS TO MAMA

1972   139
1973   150
1974   187

Epilogue   217

PART ONE

THE CALLING

CHAPTER ONE

RIDING TO A TEXAS COURTHOUSE in support of an imprisoned McMillan male relative was old hat to nearly every passenger in the vehicle but me. For me, it was a first. The person of our pointed concern that wintry day was my only son, Ohene. It was a cloudy, chilly January morning in 2006. My nephew, Chavis, drove his hulking SUV, navigating the toll roads from Richardson, a northern suburb of Dallas, toward the courthouse in Fort Worth. I rode shotgun as my three sisters, Karen, Jackie, and Kathy, and my mother Eva filled the two rows of seats behind us.

Later that morning, we joined other relatives in a busy-bodied courtroom on the fifth floor of the Tarrant County criminal courthouse. When we entered, they were already seated, sitting in a restrained yet spirited tension. There was Ohene's wife Chaka and her mother Ireatha. Felicia, Ohene's mother and my ex-wife, was with her mother Oretha. Nearby was one of Ohene's sisters, born through Felicia's second marriage. Felicia's brother, Tim, was also there. Together, we managed to fill the first two rows of corner seats near the empty jury box.

After what felt like hours, Ohene finally entered the room handcuffed, wearing dingy jailhouse coveralls, escorted by his attorney and a uniformed bailiff. Ohene's presence began to penetrate the slow but steady stream of seemingly unrelated transactions and stifled conversations between courtroom players and the many scattered, concerned families—who, like us, were trying valiantly to suppress their anxieties and fears under the scrutiny of cameras and the panning eyes of uniformed and plainclothes law enforcement officials. A surprising wave of energy filled the room with Ohene's every step and seemed to capture us all at once: newspapers among his family members folded and disappeared, conversations between us ceased, and our fragmented tribe—thrust together for this stunning moment—froze. Our sudden shift into a concentrated focus quietly rippled through the courtroom, as if a judge had struck his mighty gavel, calling everyone to order. This, however, was not the case.

None of us knew it then, but weeks later Ohen would plead guilty to mail fraud, be sentenced to eighteen months in a minimum security prison, and be required to pay a nonsensical fine of $300,000. He had been tempted by a "fast money" scheme and paid dearly for his error. Once he had served his time, Ohene would later rejoin his family and lovingly co-parent his son, Dakar Nasir.

But that would happen later. That day, Ohene's eyes darted everywhere in the room but toward us. When he finally looked our way, he visibly scanned each face of his extended family quickly, one by one. Seeing my son this way was enough to drive a stake into my side. The scene was all too recognizable, so familiar, yet eerie and strange at the same time. For I, too, once stood where Ohene now stood and the instantaneous recognition of that image swept me up and away.

My thoughts raced wildly. My mind's eye rose above the rail that separated spectators from the courtroom officers. It felt as though my entire being was rising over that divider, gliding toward the bench, carrying me directly in front of the judge. Now the eyes of my sisters, my mother, and the strangers within the room were upon me, standing in handcuffs and chains, in white prison coveralls, before another judge, in another dimension. I turned to see nearly these same faces, unrecognizable at first, appearing as they were years younger, wrapped in a similar tender, loving gaze as the one they had bestowed upon my only son. But now their interwoven mix of pain and love was directed upon me.

It was another time, and another place. No longer this cloudy, damp

January day in 2006. It was July 1968, more than a year before Ohene's birth even, thirty-eight years and six months further back in time. I was now reliving a dry, hot summer day in what is now the Frank Crowley Courts Building, less than a quarter mile from where President John F. Kennedy was assassinated five years earlier. I stood before Judge James Zimmermann and received my final sentencing: ten years confinement in the Texas Department of Corrections for "the malicious destruction of private property over the value of $50." I was led from that courtroom by a squad of deputy sheriffs, one of whom gleefully whispered in my ear that "a pine box was waiting on me" at the Ellis Prison Unit. I turned away from him and raised my fists in the air in a salute to a courtroom filled with family, friends, comrades, and the curious. The next day, the *Dallas Morning News*' front-page article announced, "A Shouting McMillan Jailed."

By the late spring of 1968, just weeks after the murder of Dr. Martin Luther King, Jr. at the Lorraine Hotel in Memphis, Tennessee, my mother referred to that white, windowless eight-story building, which housed the county jail and the criminal courts, as my second home. Many of my fellow Dallas SNCC members and I had been paraded in and out of that building—as well as the city jail and the municipal and justice of the peace courts. This was an attempt at what we would later have concrete verification of: what we instinctively knew then as the federal government's national and strategic campaign to "disrupt and destroy" the Black liberation movement.

In fact, that counterintelligence plan (known as COINTELPRO) was aimed at any and all actual, emerging, promising, or potentially progressive anti-war, anti-racist, and anti-imperialist formations within the United States. The driving force of the official arm of "white backlash" was the FBI, led by J. Edgar Hoover, the very person who began his climb to near irresistible force back in 1919 as the chief of monitoring and disrupting the work of "radicals" such as Marcus Garvey, Emma Goldman, and even US Supreme Court Justice Felix Frankfurter.

But that appearance in front of Judge Zimmermann wasn't the end. More like another beginning. What turned out to be my most pivotal arrest—the mother of all arrests—took place in March 1969 after I made bond on the ten-year conviction for destruction of private property, and three months before I became an outlaw on the run. It was a massive, synchronized raid by the combined forces of federal (FBI, ATF), state (Texas Rangers), county (sheriffs), and city police, utilizing street closings, helicopters, and dogs to strike three of our SNCC houses at once. This included our home base office in the West Dallas housing projects, our central office in a South Dallas house on Peabody Street, and my home in a two-bedroom Oak Cliff apartment, which Felicia and I shared with Ed Harris (aka "Black Ed") and his wife. The raid took place around 5:00 AM.

I had been in bed for not more than an hour. My eyes had barely closed. I entered sleep for just a few moments when loud breaking noises and shouts crashed through my skull, shaking me awake. I heard voices screaming "Police! Police! Throw down your weapons!" and "You're under arrest!" I am not sure how they entered the apartment—with a key, a battering ram, or what. They stormed through our only entrance, in the living room. I jumped to my feet, dressed in only my underwear, grabbed the thirty-caliber carbine near the bed, and ran to the closed bedroom door. Felicia was sitting up in the bed now, asking, "What is it?" I slowly opened the door, the rifle stock on my right hip and my left hand on the doorknob.

I cracked it open slowly and saw Ed's bedroom door also opening. He was holding a pistol and looked into my eyes for a quick second, a puzzled look on his face. With our bodies still within our respective rooms, we turned our heads toward the noise to see the living room filling with police; most were crouching near the floor, some were moving slowly toward the kitchen with their backs along the walls. They had guns— rifles, pistols, and shotguns—pointed at us. They paused for a moment at the sight of our heads sticking out of our rooms and my rifle leveling toward them. I quickly recoiled back into the room and loaded a round into the chamber.

My heart hammered against my chest. Shock waves seemed to flash through my hands. I lowered the gun toward the bedroom door I had left ajar. Felicia was standing near me, her arms across my shoulders, her body pressing against mine. The shouts from the living room erupted again. "Throw down your weapons! Lay down the rifle!" I slowly opened the door. I could see Ed once again. His expression was one of incensed, determined rage. He shouted, "What are you motherfuckers doing? You pigs had better get back! Get back!" Black Ed and I were only a nod away from stepping out and opening fire upon these invaders. Felicia's mouth moved closer to my ear. With her hands pressed on my shoulder, she whispered almost inaudibly at first. I was only half hearing her. Then, raising her voice a little more, in a stronger tone, I heard Felicia say, "I'm carrying your son. I'm pregnant, Ernest, and I'm carrying your son."

I turned to her to see the tears spilling down her lovely face and the truth of her words roaring through her eyes. I looked again toward Ed. We exchanged no words. I passed the rifle through the door, its nozzle toward the ceiling, and lowered it to the floor. Ed looked at me again. His astonishment faded into a knowing resignation. Seconds later, all four of us, me, Ed, and our wives, were in varying stages of dress, from underwear to nightgowns, sitting on the couch. Ed and I were hand-cuffed from behind, while our "rights" were quoted to us, our weapons on display as trophies.

The apartment quickly filled with more unwanted guests. Armed men swarmed through the living room and the bedrooms. There were at least two dozen in our tiny apartment. Some were forced into the kitchen by their sheer numbers, as there was no space for them to stand or move otherwise. One of the uniformed men pressed his face inches from mine, his lips wagging yet the meaning of his words, the sounds emitting from his lips, failing to register. The frenzy was on, pistols and rifles swung here and there. Some smiled with glee, others squinted their eyes while roaming the conquered apartment, and some bounced on their toes, clearly pumped for the "big game" and looking for some ass to kick.

Though we were all seated on the couch, our arms pinned to our backs, our wrists laced in steel cuffs, to them we were a dangerous, captured prey. I trembled as an angry electrical force raced through my body, shooting from my head to my toes. I heard voices from these officers, but their voices sounded distant and muffled. I am sure they were shouting and cursing, because their eyes bulged and their veins strained against their skins, but I heard little. Ed's voice, Felicia's words, the touch of her skin pressed by my side—such a steady pressure. These sounds and touches were present and distinct, while the sounds and images of the invaders blurred and faded.

It was at that moment that I knew. I knew all the actions my comrades and I had been taking up to this point were of a fantasy dream world. We had been actors in a play, while these officers were real, ready to kill, seriously prepared to do whatever it took to wipe us out of this picture, this world ripe with revolution and change. Until that moment, I was a romantic, a dreamer acting at revolution, playing at rebellion, and going by a script that these goons never read or fathomed.

Never again would I be the Ernest McMillan I had been before. This struggle was no longer about my life and freedom, and that of those around the country. This was all so real and very personal now. I was going to be a father and my son-to-be had literally saved our lives!

It would be many months before I could ever fully sleep through the night. My body would only drift into sleep after I saw the sun safely rise into the sky. I was resolved, perhaps more unconsciously than anything else, never to sleep a full night ever again.

CHAPTER TWO

DALLAS'S SKYLINE CAN BE SEEN on a clear day or night, from twenty-five miles away while driving on the road. It is an especially remarkable heavenly vision driving in from the east, as I did several times traveling home from the Mississippi Delta in 1979 and 1980. That panorama, rising above the darkened highway before my near-snoozing eyes, served as a recharging kick to the senses. Nearing the city limits, a large sign on the shoulder of the road, proudly sponsored by the ultra-conservative John Birch Society, welcomed you to Dallas, my hometown—"The City of Excellence." At this point, the lanes of the highway would begin to multiply from two to four as you neared the city's heart. The streets were clean, wide, and well-lit, and the buildings ultra-modern.

During the late 1970s and early '80s, Dallas ranked as the country's seventh-largest city. It boasted of being the site of the world's largest airport, the country's largest state fairgrounds, and possessing the tallest buildings west of the Mississippi. Since its founding in 1841, Dallas was always a major hub for industry. First it was cotton, then banking, wholesale trade, and high-tech manufacturing. Dallas has long attracted people and business for its commercial activities, convention facilities, sporting and cultural events. To many, the city dazzles through its architecture, thriving commerce, affluence, glitter, and pomp. As the saying goes, however, all that glitters isn't gold. In a very real way, Dallas' impressive steel and concrete entombed the blood, limbs, muscle, and sinew of its growing Brown and Black population.

I was born in 1945 and grew up in a section of Dallas that was less than a five-minute walk from the edges of downtown and known by many monikers—North Dallas, Short North Dallas, and Freedman's Town. The city and area businesses often advertised my community as being "in the shadows of downtown Dallas," but for me, it glistened with light. This was the heart of Black Dallas.

My tight-knit neighborhood was bounded by downtown on the south and southwest, by Maple Avenue on the west, McKinney Avenue to the north, and Haskell Avenue to the east. Our nearest neighbors to the west were residents of Little Mexico, which encompassed working-class homes and a housing project. To our north resided the more affluent whites (near and around Turtle Creek), while to our south and east was a strange mix of aristocratic whites, with their large, mansion-like homes, and working-class whites.

Our Black town within the city contained two cab companies, a theater, a public library, hotels, rooming houses, community centers, barbershops, shoe and electrical repair shops, grocery stores, restaurants (including barbecue houses, chicken shacks, and fish markets), laundries, medical clinics, drug stores, a hospital (with doctors, nurses, beds, and a pharmacy), liquor stores, bars, shine parlors, dance halls, night clubs, hotels, newspapers, business offices, real estate agencies, churches, schools, and service stations. The YMCA, local NAACP, and even the Progressive Voters' League headquartered there as well.

For nineteen years, my family and I lived in a house at 2316 Allen Street wedged between two of the neighborhood's main streets—Thomas Avenue and State Street. Walking south from our home on Allen Street you'd cross an alley, a frame house, then a dry cleaner, a family restaurant, a pool hall, and a liquor store, before reaching Thomas Avenue. The alley adjacent to our home was a drinking and stash spot for the corner winos, a convenient shortcut for many, and a playground for neighborhood kids.

Some mornings I'd find our trash can moved from the rear of the house and mysteriously replaced underneath our bathroom window. It did not take me long to figure out that Peeping Toms were using the trash can, standing on it to peer into our bathroom most likely when one of my sisters would bathe.

In some ways, it was another world that ran parallel to Thomas—a major artery for the adult world. The alley was a space shared mainly by the kids and the winos, but for me it was my main drag, a spot in which I knew practically every detail of this eight-block-long "boulevard."

One of my favorite rituals during my early adolescence to the pre-teen years was playing "army." We played it during the summer days and many evenings throughout the school year. High season was summer-time, when up to thirty of us neighborhood boys would gather and choose sides. In a matter of minutes, mock guerrilla warfare would break out. Old, abandoned cars became tanks, underground sewers became bunkers and pillboxes, empty beer bottles became grenades, and the tall grasses in vacant lots became rice paddies.

Sometimes, and especially when there were just enough to form one army, we would become a curse to the winos. We would set up ambushes, giving bird calls as signals while lying in wait for a tipsy drunk to take a swig or two and then stash the remaining liquor for later. If we were around, however, there would never be a "later," for we'd usually empty its contents and return the bottle to its hiding spot, sometimes with a bold note declaring that the wino had been struck by the "ghost brigade."

Several years passed before I realized that we—Black and Brown boys—were acting out what we were seeing in movies and on television. We were pretending, but war was real, had been for our fathers and grand-fathers. In the name of the USA and the very flag I pledged allegiance to in school every morning, death and destruction rained upon countless thousands, people who too often were impoverished folks simply defend-ing their homeland against foreign invaders—us.

Thomas Avenue dead-ended into the newly built Central Expressway that cut the neighborhood in two. The highway ripped through homes, businesses, the freedmen's burial grounds, and displaced thousands. Before that destruction, this tightly compressed area thrived. For new arrivals—Black folk from East Texas farms, Arkansas cotton fields, and Louisiana plantations—the corner of Hall Street and Thomas Avenue was a magnet to find resources and connections to chart new lives.

•

My family were not strictly "race people." They were not Garveyites, or Black Muslims for that matter. The Partee side of my clan—especially my mother, her twin sister, and my uncles Cecil and Clifton—held more of an expressed affinity for DuBois, Robeson, Thurgood Marshall, and Ida Delaney; men and women who advocated and fought for justice and equality right here and right now. Those on the McMillan side were more Biblical, non-racial expressionists, though my dad and his brother and their parents would not refrain from using terms like "crackers" and "rednecks." My dad would often remind me to cut off the light when not in use so as to "get the white man out of my pocket."

It was the Partees who would have discussions about the state of things and avidly read literature and talk about current events. They would not oppose or chastise the work of an all-Black this or a separatist that but used their time and energies to sharpen and equip themselves and the community for fair treatment and dignity. Enlightenment. Kahlil Gibran. Classic literature. Ancient mythology. History.

Mom, through a cruel twist of fate, was not able to pursue the same rich, post–high school education as her older brothers and sisters. Therefore she and her twin sister NeNe were always engaging themselves in rigorous educational pursuits. Always learning. Our home became an oasis for stimulating thinking and curiosity. It was not unusual for our family nights, even among extended family, to be filled with quizzes and robust competitions—from naming the state capitals, playing Twenty Questions, or Animal, Vegetable or Mineral? to presenting family-created skits, recording songs, and performing recitals with an old 78 rpm record player. We played odd card games like canasta and Fan-Tan. Mom and her sisters prided themselves as excellent bridge players, too.

The Partees and the McMillans were also a rich and colorful blend of city life on one side and country life on the other—community activism on one and church activism on the other. Where these families aligned was in the valuing of hard work, education, and professionalism.

At one time, Aunt Neva, my mother's identical twin sister, lived with us. My dad's parents—a prominent physician and socialite—lived two doors down in one of the neighborhood's largest homes, and my mother's father, a farmer, moved to the city in his final years and lived a few blocks down the street. My mother's two brothers, Uncle Cecil, a renowned teacher, and Uncle Clifton, a bachelor and activist, visited often, while my dad's brother, Walter, lived next door with my grandparents. As my grandfather, Dr. McMillan, grew older, his medical practice continued in their home for several years.

Though I had no brothers, my cousin Harry and two older first cousins, Harrison "Tookie" Partee-Taylor and Michael McMillan, were my idols. My sisters Karen, Jackie, and Kathy were buddies, and allies often enough, but, at times, pesky thorns in my side. Karen, the first-born and two years my senior, had her own peers and associates. Jackie was a year younger than me and my best friend during most of my formative years. We would climb trees, race each other, and play games together. Jackie even commanded the enemy troops with my toy soldiers when we would battle it out on the porch or in the yard. My sister Kathy was eight years younger than I was. She was the "miracle child," having been born despite the fact my mother had had her tubes tied nearly a decade earlier. My dad would proudly boast about his prowess in overcoming those physical barriers to his semen, but it was more likely due to faulty surgery. Kathy was relegated most of her early years to being the baby of the family. She intended on escaping that role as often as possible and sought to play and hang out with her older siblings.

We were preacher's kids. Daddy was one of the first Blacks to attend Perkins School of Theology at Southern Methodist University. He participated in a pilot program created by the dean and trustees, aimed at making a smooth, orderly, painstaking road to desegregate the school. Dad was one of a handful of Black Methodist men selected based on one notable criterion: they had to be mature, married men with families. I presume this was a well-calculated formula to offset fears of race mixing, especially the danger of sexual relations between Black men and white women. In addition to being a part-time minister, my dad held various jobs, including postal worker, adult educator at a night school, even elevator operator at a downtown business establishment. He wound up unable to study diligently and got poor grades. He also could not adjust to the level of segregation and paternalistic approaches and either flunked out or dropped out after a semester at SMU. I never knew for sure.

Daddy was first a pastor at the original St. Luke United Methodist Church in Dallas. It was a small one-room building then. He was eventually transferred to a church in Corsicana, about an hour and a half's drive south from Dallas. He had a parsonage there and would sometimes spend weekends in the small town. Mama was never the consummate church wife or "first lady" and Daddy never insisted on the unwritten, traditional behaviors of pastors' wives because he himself had broken the pledge he had made prior to his wedding vows that he would never become a preacher. Though he professed to answering a calling, she probably felt it was more his mother's ongoing, nagging insistence he become a church leader, his desire to please her, and the pressures of becoming more high-ranked socially that tilted the scale, winning his tug-of-war of career choices.

My dad wasn't a conventional preacher, either. He was no great orator. He did not whoop and holler in the pulpit like most Southern preachers. He loved the Apostle Paul's writings and came across as a soft-spoken teacher or philosopher when he preached. I often went to sleep during his sermons and was secretly embarrassed for him, hoping he would develop a more flamboyant or captivating style like the celebrated Rev. I.B. Loud, who led our family church, St. Paul United Methodist. It would be decades before I understood and appreciated how my father enjoyed the pastoral role of building relationships and counseling people more than preaching.

Come to think of it, we were quite the unconventional Black church family. Sure, we children exhibited "good home training," but other than Daddy, none of us carried bibles, or read them much beyond Sunday services. Mom did not cook meals for the congregation, sing in the church choir, politic for Daddy, or perform any traditional duties expected of a preacher's wife. Ironically, too, perhaps, that other than the habitual now-I-lay-me-down-to-sleep prayer at bedtime, I did not learn prayer from my parents. It was my paternal grandmother, whom we called "Mud Dear," who drilled her grandkids and demanded prayer for nearly every occasion. If she felt moved to give us a dime or a quarter, she would hold it and our hands together in hers, and say a prayer to bless it.

I was Mud Dear's errand boy, her servant. She would prepare me for the next chore or errand by saying, "I'm gonna *let* you do something for me." In her later years, she was so big and heavy that she could not move. In fact, she was almost incapacitated, but she always brought prayer to everything.

During her marriage, she and grandpa—Dr. McMillan—attended two different churches. She was a member of Bethel Christian Methodist Episcopal and he of St. Paul United Methodist Church; both were founded in the late 1800s by former enslaved families. These two churches were only two blocks apart. Mud Dear sang in the choir at Bethel and Grandpa was a trustee at St. Paul. Their acceptance and mutual understanding of this arrangement endured as pillars in their marriage.

My faith wavered at a young age and it all began with a tornado. There had been weather alerts, and everyone gathered around the television. It was scary. When my bedtime arrived, I did not want to go to my room, for fear we might be swept away. As the winds were gusting outside, I was filled with fear and apprehension, especially given I was in a room by myself. Daddy came to check on me and I told him that I could not sleep because of the impending tornado. He sat on my bed and said, "Son, God loves you. He never makes tornadoes happen at night. Don't be afraid."

Months later, a tornado *did* hit at night. I was so angry with my father that this incident made me question my entire faith. In my young mind, he had lied to me. A minister had lied to me. I was blind to understanding that he meant to console and comfort his young son rather than deceive me.

•

I think we all go through a period in our lives when we question things and rebel. Individuation: I did that early. From the age of six to ten, I would climb up on the roof of Mud Dear's house at night to see the streets, hear the people talking, and enjoy the night sky. To get on the roof, I would walk to her house, go up the outside steps, and then climb on the top rail to the roof. Theirs was one of the larger two-story homes in the neighborhood.

My dog, Sonny, would follow me. Sonny was a dirty blond mutt with yellow teeth and a tail that curled up into a backward C. I adored him, but he proved to be a pain in the ass to my Uncle Walter. For some reason, Sonny became public enemy number one, and, to this day, it was unjustifiable. Maybe the complaint was fleas or ticks, or maybe it was because Sonny would dig a hole or two at the edge of Mud Dear's house and use it as refuge from the hot summer sun. Whatever the reason, Uncle Walter was determined to get rid of my dog.

The showdown came one evening when he had Sonny trapped under the house with a dogcatcher (or some henchman) assisting him, unsuccessfully attempting to get Sonny to come out to his waiting leash. I could not believe it! While they tried to corral Sonny on one side of the house,

I went to the other side and called for him. Sonny quickly crawled out to me, and we were off and running toward the streets. Uncle Walter and the dogcatcher gave chase. It must have been quite a scene. The guys near the pool hall and the corner liquor store saw a boy and a dog being chased by two grown men and began hollering cheers of "Go, boy!" and "Run!"

We swerved through the throngs and got away. After a few hours, when things died down and there was no sign of my uncle, I eased back home and sneaked Sonny inside, onto our back porch. On the way home, a couple of the corner regulars were sympathetic and even offered to "take care" of Uncle Walter. I just kept walking, eyes down, focused on Sonny without acknowledging them. We managed to get through that adventure to live another day, and Uncle Walter never tried that again.

•

I had no idea that our family was "poor" even though we lived in a tiny home next to my grandparents' mansion-like house. Even though there would be days when the cold winter air could find its way inside our house through its many cracks and crevices, and we would often stick cloth in the cracks to fend off the chill, such was no big deal. Even though there would be times we were without running water, having been cut off by the water company for late payment. Hey, it was fun sometimes to run a hose from grandma's house to ours and fill up the buckets with water for bathing and washing! Though we never ventured to fancy restaurants or other such places, never had mad rags to wear or regular spending allowances, the notion of being poor was not a concept I could relate to myself or my family in any way. We were rich in so many other ways.

Even before my dad left home, having "fallen in love with long distance" and moved to Atlanta, it was natural for every able body in the house to work and bring home some bacon—*something*. My first job was working the neighborhood paper route when I was ten. By high school,

I moved up the corporate ladder, taking on jobs as an usher and popcorn maker at the State Theater. Later, I worked as a dishwasher at a cafeteria, was eventually promoted to bus boy, and finally the ultimate service gig— banquet waiter by my senior year at Booker T. Washington High School.

Being poor and thinking poor are two distinctly separate things. Growing up in a loving, secure, and supportive home and in a virtually intact, nearly self-sustaining neighborhood can allow one to consider all basic needs fulfilled, as indeed they were. In fact, there was no such thing as "needs" within my childhood. My world was playing, eating, sleeping, running errands, visiting friends and neighbors, and going to school. Once that was done, a new day came, bringing with it a new round of the same great cycle of life: playing, eating, sleeping, running errands, on and on. But I was in for a rude awakening.

I was shocked and embarrassed to find a charitable box containing canned groceries and a whole turkey on our doorstep one November afternoon. While I and other members of Booker T.'s National Honor Society conducted our annual community project of distributing Thanksgiving food baskets to the needy, somehow my family was listed among the "less fortunate" and became a recipient of a gift basket by some anonymous charity!

Allen Street was the only home I knew until I became an adult. Allen Street and this segregated Black community was my incubator and my incinerator, the source whereby my essential being was pressed, hammered, and roasted until that fateful day my wings emerged and I dared to fly.

CHAPTER THREE

BY THE EARLY 1960s, DALLAS was a big-league city with a fiercely backward-looking Establishment. At least one of the two daily newspapers alternately called for the restoration of the death penalty, the abolition of the United Nations, the end of government welfare programs, and the return to the "good ol' days." It was not highly unusual for the Texas courts to enthusiastically mete out prison sentences in the thousands of years or "life and one day" to Black offenders. This practice made those who were being accused of a third felony conviction plead guilty to sentences of more than a dozen years to avoid an automatic life imprisonment sentence.

The police force was nearly all white. The few Black cops were prohibited from arresting any white person. There were about one hundred thousand arrests per year, mainly of Blacks and Mexicans. Even the ambulance system was segregated. White companies were only permitted to pick up and carry white bodies to the hospitals or morgue. The city's schools and neighborhoods continued to be rigidly segregated.

Dallas' response to the Supreme Court's school order to desegregate at "all deliberate speed" was to adopt a "stair-step" plan: one grade per year, beginning at kindergarten, and all the while honoring the blatantly segregated neighborhood configurations. So by the 1970s, a generation after the order was rendered, very few visible changes could be detected. Elected officials were handpicked by the white Citizens'

Council. Developers loved scripting and orchestrating Dallas' economic policies and land use system practices. For example, the actual policy touted as "urban renewal" effectively shaped the city's geography as urban removal.

The ugly spirit of Dallas spoke for itself repeatedly: Adlai Stevenson, the US Ambassador to the United Nations, was spat upon by an agitated white mob, Kennedy's brain was spattered upon Elm Street, and innocent Black and Brown young men such as Michael Morehead and Santos Rodriguez were slaughtered in cold blood and without any justifiable or reasonable cause.

Any casual traveler to Dallas, an elite white suburbanite or a card-carrying Klansman, would likely applaud or affirm its claim of being a "City of Excellence." To them, this was an orderly, clean, and bustling place. Yet the average resident, especially those poor, working people, and particularly people of color who resided in the shadows of Dallas, would scoff and burn with rage at the city's blind arrogance and utter hypocrisy.

•

By 1961, life became less simple for me. Growing up, being the only male child in the house, I always had a room to myself or slept in the den. When Daddy left and moved to Atlanta, I was the only male remaining at 2316 Allen Street and was, as a result, given the room in the back, along with a .32 automatic from Mama and Aunt Neva, to protect the home. My sister Karen had moved to Atlanta as well, to attend Clark College. This was a wholly new nest for the McMillans.

During this time of familial and societal upheaval, something seemed to be in the air. Was it change? My coming maturation? Or fear and anxiety, coupled with excitement? I began to gravitate to powerful messages and messengers within my community, like Rev. I. B. Loud and my high school principal, Dr. John Leslie Patton. Rev. Loud proved to be one of the most inspiring orators I had ever witnessed. Dr. Patton, as principal of Booker T. Washington High School, was a true intellectual and trail-blazer. By 1942, he developed the first Negro History Month program in Texas. He held "fireside" chats with the students that managed to be both personal and thought-provoking. Dr. Patton knew how to build us up, especially in those times of segregation and growing unrest. When he spoke, you could hear a cat walking on cotton. It was obvious to me that he preferred being a teacher first and administrator second.

In high school, I was active with the NAACP Youth Council. There were several events—council meetings as well as social and fundraising events—I would participate in. But what was most impactful for me were those more direct-action campaigns for justice and equality, like the one that finally changed the State Fair of Texas' segregated policies by the time I was in high school.

For decades, the State Fair was a major issue in the Black community. We were banned from participating in nearly all events and regulated to only one day—"Negro Achievement Day"—out of what was a month-long engagement. I felt the restriction as a stinging personal offense because my birthday, October 6, was one I could not celebrate at the State Fair grounds on the rides or in the arcades.

In 1955, the NAACP, led by activist Juanita Craft, initiated boy-cotts, legal proceedings, and closed-door negotiations to promote direct action and bring the message home to Dallas that a new day was in order. Typically, Negro Achievement Day began with a parade led by the two "colored only" high school bands and their majorettes and drill teams. In 1961, an astonishing thing happened to launch the largest protest: the bands leading the crowds into the fairgrounds stopped short of entering at the front gates. With that dramatic stoppage, the protest was on. I believe that action caused that to be the last year of a segregated State Fair of Texas.

I actively participated in organized public protests during my high school years as a NAACP Youth Council member. During that time, our targets were the segregated downtown movie theaters—The Palace and

The Majestic Theater. Those theaters only allowed Blacks seating in the balconies or "the crow's nest," while the whites were given the open-auditorium seating downstairs. Over the course of several months, on Sunday afternoons after church, we would line up in an orderly fashion in front of The Majestic Theater, dressed in our Sunday best. We would "stand-in" for hours there in an orderly fashion, approach the ticket counter, one by one, and ask for admission with money in hand. We would be denied entrance, and without fanfare or verbal exchange, we would return to the end of the line and start the process over and over again.

The summer of my junior year, I won a scholarship to attend a National Science Foundation Seminar at Prairie View A&M College, near Houston. I was excited to attend. I loved the idea of getting away from Dallas for a few weeks, being on a college campus, living in a dorm, meeting new people—especially new girls. At sixteen, I was under the spell of *Playboy* magazine and the image of a man surrounded by beautiful women who were attracted to his sophistication and worldliness, his smooth style and demeanor. I was infatuated by the Bunnies, with their ample, luscious bodies, and the prospects of "getting it on."

I was new to the world of sex. I often visited our neighborhood public library—the Paul Laurence Dunbar Library—to read action novels and any book I could find on anatomy, particularly of the naked female body. I wanted to see pussy! I had girlfriends but had little success in going all the way with any of them. I was ignorant and over-sensitive about relationships.

I was also a romantic. I loved the romantic songs of Sam Cooke, the Impressions, Jerry Butler, even Johnny Mathis. I was getting a taste for jazz, and the downtown library was my hangout on many Saturdays, listening to and checking out LPs. I was haunted by the sounds of the Chico Hamilton Quintet, Earl Garner, Earl Hines, Dave Brubeck, Nat King Cole, and others. *Playboy* became my guide to music and the arts, too. If *Playboy* said somebody was cool to listen to, then I would have to check out the artist for myself. The reviews by music critics like Nat Hentoff became my early guide through the jazz world. My mission at sixteen was to be cool, *Playboy* cool.

Prairie View, located just about an hour north of Houston, was a four-hour bus ride from Dallas. The campus was right off the highway and, as I recall, there was no bus terminal. The bus driver would just pull over and you would get off and walk to the center of the campus, which was at least a mile or two away.

I had a couple of relatives who worked or studied there. My uncle Lemon McMillan was a well-known campus administrator. I also learned that my "uncle" Ed Swinton would be there that summer working on an advanced degree. He was a teacher and a coach in Dallas Public Schools. Ed was not kin by blood. He and his wife Gwen were just very close friends of our family. So close that they became Uncle Ed and Aunt Gwen. I looked forward to seeing him around. I imagined he would be a great resource if any problems arose. I was feeling optimistic.

I arrived at my dorm room, only to learn that I was the first one there. There were four bunk beds, so I had first choice on sleeping arrangements. There was a bathroom, a couple of chairs, and one or two tables. I selected a bottom bunk near a window, placing my bags on the bed. I decided to leave the dorm to look around "the yard," so I left my *Playboy* magazine, a carton of Kool cigarettes, and my silver-handled umbrella on the table and stepped outside. The campus seemed drab, almost lifeless, and I was let down. I had anticipated walking into a colorful, exciting, dynamic center of young adult life.

Returning to the dorm room, I discovered a full house. All my new roomies had arrived along with a few others. They looked at me strangely, as if I were a ghost or alien. I soon discovered they were all wondering who I, a guy who smoked Kool cigarettes, read *Playboy*, and carried an umbrella with a silver, wolf's head-shaped handle—would turn out to be. From that moment, I was transformed through the eyes of my new peers. Much to my surprise, I was labeled what I had long wanted to be: the smooth-hero-lover-debonair-smart guy. Whatever I did or said was pretty much accepted as gospel. That summer, I learned that image often exceeds reality. For the first time in my life, I was cool.

My summer at Prairie View was opening so many new doors for me. I began to see not only myself but the world in a new way. In science, I discovered physicists and chemists like Fermi, Bohr, Einstein, Curie, and Planck. I learned modern concepts about matter and energy. The one thing that blew me away the most was a new sense of understanding that matter and energy are interchangeable. That energy cannot be destroyed, only transformed.

Today, I realize that something began to shift in my worldview that would soon burst forth into a total shift in my being. For me, these scientific discoveries clearly illustrated the existence of God or God-like energy inherent within the universe. It struck me unlike any Sunday sermon, biblical reading, or scripture ever did or possibly could ever do. I was transformed intellectually and spiritually. This was the beginning of the restoration of my faith.

For the close of the summer seminar, each student had to produce an exhibit for the science fair. I had no idea what I would do. Some of my classmates were arranging litmus tests, colorful charts, elaborate papers with illustrations, and some even conducted laboratory experiments. I finally stumbled upon an idea that would involve the transformation of living things through chemistry and/or physics. I developed an experiment using a rooster and a hen. I became the evil scientist McMillanstein and for more than three weeks, I injected testosterone (the male sex hormone) into the hen, and estrogen (the female hormone) into the rooster. The goal was to change the secondary sex characteristics of the chickens.

By the end of my experiment, the rooster, whom I dubbed George, became "Georgia," and the hen, Georgia, became "George."

My summer at Prairie View stretched me in more ways than I could have ever imagined. I opened my mind and my heart and had the time of my life. I got into a crazy scrape in Uncle Ed's car and fell in love with a fine and intelligent girl from Galveston, Alfreda Lockett, whom I would never see again. Thus began a series of significant defining moments that would shape my transition into the real world.

•

I still find it hard to believe that for most of my childhood and even my teenage years, I dreamed of being a soldier. Playing army all those years in the backyard and throughout the neighborhood was the practice I would need in becoming a real soldier, a mercenary, or even a soldier of fortune. I orchestrated many guerilla army adventures during this time. My friends and I would gather and wage tactical warfare in the alleys, behind the houses, on the roofs, over the fences and into the trees for hours at a time. Sometimes, we would even march to Turtle Creek, about a mile from our homes, and venture into that jungle land of trees, bushes, streams, and water tunnels to wage more elaborate and fantastic war scenes. Some would jump into the creek and swim after a battle. One hot summer afternoon, while on one of our routine hikes to Turtle Creek, a sizable group of our army—maybe fifteen boys, a few of them Mexicans from the Little Mexico neighborhood—were interrupted by a police patrol car with two uniformed cops. They got out of their vehicle to check to see what kind of "weapons" we were packing. Once they were assured that we were only playing with toy guns, they teased us about our game, and then issued a stern warning to behave.

In high school, I joined our ROTC's cadet program, the National Defense Cadet Corps (NDCC), and the drill team. Our drill team was one of the best in the state. We twirled our rifles, had fancy military steps, and participated in street parades, high school football games, and other special events. I remember participating in a halftime performance at a college football game at the world-famous Cotton Bowl at Fair Park in South Dallas. Somehow, we were caught in the middle of a skirmish between the two combating teams as they exited the field. Helmets and fists were flying all around. The scuffles lasted for several minutes. Some of our cadets had to use their own helmets and M-1 rifles for protection or retaliation against anyone breaking into our ranks.

My first year, I started as a buck private. I rose steadily in rank each successive year, from squad leader to platoon leader by my sophomore year. I eventually became an instructor colonel and leader of the drill team in my senior year. I even dreamed of going to West Point one day. For a time, I enjoyed the role, the status, and the work that came along with such a position.

The previous year's drill team commander, Robert Wesson, was the best. Six years later, he would marry my sister Karen and become my brother-in-law. Prior to Wesson's command, we were ranked maybe the third best of Dallas' three Black high school male drill teams. By the time he graduated, we had become the second-best drill team in the entire state. Our school rivaled only the best outfit in Dallas: Lincoln High School's Black Knights. They were too cold—dressed in all black, making slow-stepping struts and highly precise moves. Their mere presence owned such an air of dignity and charisma. They were impressive!

As it turned out, I could lead a pretend army of guerrilla fighters through the neighborhood, but not a group of high school ROTC cadets. Not only did we fail in finally becoming the number one team in Dallas, and thus Texas, we fell another notch or two under my tenure. I was not as detail-oriented as Robert, nor did I have good command of instruction. I also lacked the ability to build confidence in the cadets. Robert would create intricate movements from simple steps, basic patterns that would magically evolve into beautifully choreographed wonders. I was just barking and giving commands. So much was missing in my leadership. As a last resort, I led a makeover of our uniforms, dyeing our khaki uniforms red to complement our white helmets and white gloves and mirror our school colors. This, too, was a complete failure.

No number of cosmetic changes could save us or mask our poorer marching style and tired techniques. Soon, our ranks diminished. Under Wesson, we were a full platoon, perhaps four squads of eight men each, with a flag bearer and a master sergeant. During my stint, we were just five or six guys per squad—never more than twenty-seven cadets, including myself. I soon became irritable and impatient. I even stopped starching my cadet uniform.

Things were looking better for me academically and in other social arenas. I was president of the National Honor Society and of our senior class. Looking back, these achievements were a miracle, given I was not putting one hundred percent into my studies. The spring of '63 marked the second semester of my senior year. Many impactful things were happening in the world at this time. There was a new, youthful president; street demonstrations and uprisings in Birmingham and elsewhere; the murder of Medgar Evers in Mississippi; and the heating up of the Vietnam War and fledgling anti-war protests along with it.

Our school received interns, recent college graduates, to teach a few of our classes. One young man who taught our civics class enthralled me. In just a few short weeks, he solidified the big shift in my worldview. He led discussions and lessons on communism, totalitarianism, democracy, Africa, and so much more. He helped to open my mind and taught me how we relate to the world. With all that was happening around us at that time, I finally began to ask myself how I would fit into the world. Given my continued challenges as a leader of the schools' National Defense Cadet Corps (NDCC), I was beginning to accept more and more that the military might not be the best fit for me.

One afternoon, after practice, as we reentered the school to return our rifles and prepare to wrap things up, one of the cadets—out of pure frustration—grabbed his helmet and swung it at me, shouting, "I'm sick of this shit!" The NDCC commander, our teacher Lieutenant Sasser, intervened along with a few others. Lt. Sasser was bound to back me up and discipline the cadet, not even questioning me or what may have provoked his behavior in the first place. For me, this was a shocker. I felt terrible. I had been in a dream world all to myself, dishing out orders, making bad decisions, and calling shots without regard for processes, implications, or impact on my fellow cadets. From that day forward, my passion and zeal for the military waned. These were my last days as a military man. In just a couple years, I would find my true calling, becoming a different kind of warrior: a humanitarian, anti-war, anti-imperialist anti-racist warrior, but still fighting.

CHAPTER FOUR

AFTER GRADUATING FROM BOOKER T. WASHINGTON Technical High School, I moved to Georgia in June 1963 to stay with my dad and prepare for Morehouse College. My father was the newly assigned pastor of a Methodist church in Newnan, Georgia, a sleepy little town just south of Atlanta. Daddy was delighted that I was to attend the "Black Harvard of the South." In his eyes, living with him would serve as the perfect way to get acclimated and ready for my first year of college.

We lived in the church parsonage. I slowly began to meet and hang out with young people from the church and even a few non-churchgoers, guys who hung out at a nearby community center. I had the advantage of being the stranger in town. That combination seemed to work well with the girls but in an inverse proportion with the guys. I had to make sure any girl I showed interest in was unquestionably free and single. I also had access to my father's 1960 Ford sedan—a big plus!

The summer of '63 was a high time in my life, and as it turned out, for the whole country and perhaps the world itself. This was the summer of the March on Washington and I wanted to be a part of it. Being in Newnan, however, proved to be a volatile and unhealthy combination for me. It was here that I received my first taste of establishment power, feeling the wrath of the system due to my growing interest in the movement.

My stint in Newnan was short-lived. The walls of segregation were more boldly visible in this town. The whole place seemed to accept and rigidly abide by a racist, segregationist mentality. But the youngbloods I was meeting and becoming acquainted with were growing restless, dying for the first chance to get away from Newnan. They were fed up with the low ceiling and the tight confines.

I spoke to them about options other than just leaving the South. I spoke about the protests carried out in Dallas, of the sit-ins and demonstrations other cities like Birmingham, Little Rock, and Nashville were having. These movements taking place with young people leading the way. I shared my thoughts on the possibilities of the March on Washington, how it could increase pressure for change. I asked them in what ways we could support these strides—raise money, do a local action. Even if we could not physically go to D.C., there were things we could do in Newnan.

It did not take long before word spread beyond the audience I wanted to reach. Word got to the sheriffs and police that a troublemaker was agitating around town. Soon, deputies came to the parsonage and met with my dad. They reported that his "boy was going around causing trouble," and if he did not put a stop to it, then they would be obliged to take care of it. Daddy told me he feared for my safety, that I "didn't know these people and what they would do." He bought me a one-way train ticket back to Dallas and told me to stay there until it was time for school, and to go directly to Morehouse for freshman orientation in September. When I returned to Georgia and moved on campus that fall, Daddy was also living there, having abruptly been transferred to Atlanta, where he enrolled in Gammon Seminary.

Morehouse was a cold slap in the face, a momentous cultural shock to my senses, but I put on a nonchalant front, moving and acting as though all was par for the course. Dressing up in a blazer and tie was the daily uniform; I was to wear it to attend classes, and even to breakfast. We were mandated to attend chapel services and had designated seats in the auditorium, and someone was always there checking attendance. But those sermon/lectures were not always dull or mind-numbing, as I imagined they would be. In fact, a couple of lectures would challenge some of my own lifelong assumptions and shake up my sense of "normal thinking."

I was riveted when one distinguished clergy scholar went so far as to declare that "good" was not always good and "evil" not always evil. I recall him asking us if it was good for one to turn the other cheek if attacked. If a home invader threatened your mother's or sister's life and you stood by without drawing and using a weapon against him to protect their lives, wouldn't that be evil?

I loved the humanities class where we listened to music like Coltrane's "Africa Brass" and Miles Davis's "Sketches of Spain." The professor asked us to use our imaginations to "see" what they were saying to us. I hated my French class. The professor would call on you to respond in French to a statement or question from him spoken in French and would threaten to do bodily harm if you failed to respond correctly. The girls from nearby Spelman College intimidated me, as the ones I felt attracted to and wanted to date seemed to have some bias against me, some criteria in their own mind. They were more concerned about determining my class status, family heredity, strategic plan for prosperity and wealth than who I really was as a person.

By November of my freshman year, I was seriously wondering what I was doing there. My roommates were great; two of the three in our dormitory room in Quarles Hall were straight out of Birmingham's movement for equal rights. One was from Parker High School, the main source of student activism on the front lines of the demonstrations, facing police dogs, high-powered water hoses, billy clubs, and jail time. They minimized the dangers and the pain inflicted upon them and reminisced as if they were speaking of a party in the streets.

Then the news of JFK's assassination erupted like a tidal wave across the campus. The shift from shock and outrage morphed swiftly into anger and vengeance, and being from Dallas, I was an automatic, irrational, but obvious target for many. Soon, my roomies became my shield, as wave after wave of Morehouse men came looking for me, asking, "Where's that nigger from Dallas? They killed the President and he's gonna pay for it!"

My roomies held it down, letting no one enter the room, and told me to stay put until the madness passed. They brought me chow from the dining hall over the next three days, and only after Oswald was captured and subsequently killed was I able to return to classes and my daily routine.

With the alien Morehouse culture along with a growing restlessness, I began to spend my free time off campus. I learned that I was not alone in feeling antagonism about college life. The image of the "Morehouse Man" as privileged and arrogant was widespread within the surrounding neighborhood, where few opportunities existed for escaping the narrow pathways available to most Black men.

One night on campus, as I wrestled, unable to sleep, I heard a sound truck blasting a message that would completely alter my life's course. I went to the window and heard a message repeated over and over: a call to join the fight against segregation and to defeat Lester Maddox's violent stance against integration. Maddox was the owner of a restaurant in downtown Atlanta that had become a symbolic target because he used pick-axe handles to attack Blacks who sought to eat there. That night was also my introduction to the Student Non-Violent Coordinating Committee, or SNCC. I admired the courage and militancy I saw in the twenty-four-hour, seven-day-a-week demonstrations outside the restaurant. It was rowdy, messy, and full of spirit; so different from the orderly, well-mannered stand-ins I experienced in Dallas.

I quickly fell in step with the young men who were not content to merely walk around the restaurant clapping, chanting, and singing, but who felt and acted on the impulse to break through and crash the police line. They were members of SNCC. With them, I experienced my first movement-related arrest. We were dragged out of the restaurant and thrown in jail on a misdemeanor. While in custody, I met Dick Gregory, and other full time local activists.

After that, every chance I got I visited the SNCC national headquarters, located just a few blocks from Morehouse's campus, at 8½ Raymond Street. I was drawn there and met some of the staff, including George Mants, Jim Foreman, Julian Bond, Judy Richardson, John Lewis, and Ruby Doris Robinson. I began to feel a sense of mission, of belonging, of undisputed purpose there. By the middle of December, I was certain that this movement was what made my life whole.

SNCC was an organization of 150 field secretaries, most of whom were posted in majority Black counties throughout the "Black Belt" that was mainly made up of rural communities from North Carolina to Arkansas. We were paid a subsistence wage of $10 a week and were co-dependent on the residents and neighbors where we lived and worked. As a minor, nearly nineteen years old, I was required to have written permission from my parents to come onboard. At first, I forged their names.

I eventually sat with my dad late one evening in his home a few blocks from the Morehouse College campus. I was excited and nervous about his reaction to my request for him to sign and thereby approve of me not only joining SNCC, but also dropping out of college and leaving for some unknown destination to face new challenges and unfathomable dangers. Daddy was cool. He had a sense about where my head was at and who my new associations were. He asked if I really knew what I was in for; how mean, treacherous, and powerful the forces against Civil Rights were. He wondered out loud if I was aware or in any way prepared to risk my education, my health, even my life for this cause. I did not have an answer but managed to nod my head and mumble a word about having faith and believing everything would work out. He finally signed the papers, then looked up at me, saying, "If you really intend on doing this, then just follow your heart—but talk with your mother first."

I called Mama that same evening, and though we were nine hundred miles apart, unable to speak face to face, and without prior communication or notice from my dad or me, she provided me with essentially the same pronouncement that Dad extended. She told me, "If this is something you truly feel and are committed to carrying out, then go with it, trust your spirit and your heart's calling."

And so, with my parents' permission, I spread my wings and officially left my comfortable nest for the real world that held my destiny.

PART TWO:

MOVEMENT

CHAPTER FIVE

THE OLD SCHOOL BUS HURTLED down the bumpy, red-dirt country road, driven by a man possessed. He and I were its only occupants. It was a warm, sunny day and all the windows were open, allowing heat waves to dance over our skin. My duffle bag rolled back and forth across the aisle as Willie Ricks navigated the bus around potholes and along the swirling trenches made by trucks and tractors. Tall pine trees lined the shoulders of the road and dust blew up in a billowy trail forming a brown sea of earth around us. Over the bus engine's growls, Willie loudly recounted last night's mass meeting in Albany, the county seat of Dougherty County, to prepare for another voter registration drive. He was excited to share that his home base, Lee County, would rally to prepare for its own Freedom Day.

I sat behind him, bouncing and sliding around my seat, leaning my ear over as close as I could to catch his voice before the wind pulled it out the windows. This being my very first day in Southwest Georgia, and my first real assignment as a SNCC field secretary, I wanted to absorb as much knowledge and inside information as rapidly as possible. Suddenly, Willie was hitting the brakes and veering over to the side. "Look, a gator!" he shouted. Sure enough, I looked ahead and saw an eight- to ten-foot-long alligator dawdling across the road. In the Deep South experience ahead of me, gators would prove to be the least of my worries.

It had been a whirlwind month. I swirled from being a freshman at Morehouse College to a new full-time civil rights worker, a fresh recruit enrolled at the Dorchester Cooperative Center near Savannah, Georgia. At Dorchester, I took a crammed ten-day course, classes and workshops embracing the ideals and practices of non-violence and community organizing. Essentially, it was boot camp, a seminar on becoming an active citizen leader. Within a highly participatory, circle format, the battled-tested teachers utilized history, philosophy, civics, and their own experience to teach power structure analysis, movement strategies, and the legal and direct-action techniques for confronting power. I met and learned from people I had long heard a lot about in the news, books, and through conversations at Morehouse. They were movement leaders, like Andy Young, Ella Baker, and Rev. Hosea Williams.

Within weeks of walking the hallways at Morehouse, I was kicking up dust on the trails on my first short-lived placement as a full-time field secretary in Fort Valley, Georgia, near the Fort Valley State College (now known as Fort Valley State University) campus. To be a SNCC field secretary in the mid- to late-'60s was to join a cadre of brothers and sisters from around the country committed to enlisting others to get involved in the fight for self-determination. There were many ways to engage in transforming the South—the Mississippi Freedom Democratic Party, unions, cooperatives and more. SNCC wanted to develop the leadership capabilities latent in the hearts and minds of ordinary folk. I arrived in Fort Valley by bus and found my way to the address of Phil, the SNCC field secretary there. I was only in Fort Valley for a week or so before I learned that Phil had been summoned to the Selective Service Draft Board to submit for the massive conscription for young men to go to fight in the invasion of Vietnam. Phil obeyed that order but vowed to not be drafted under the conscious objection clause of the Selective Service Act. I was flushed with apprehension and doubted my capabilities as a young "rookie" to fill the void that would be created by Phil's absence. The SNCC leadership evidently knew full well of this abrupt distortion, and decided to temporarily close down the Fort Valley project. I soon received a call from the already legendary Charles Sherrod, then SNCC's regional director for the Southwest Georgia Project, redirecting me to SNCC's regional head-quarters in Albany, Georgia, to be assigned to a new post with existing veteran leadership. That became the beginning of my work with Willie Ricks.

Now I found myself hurtling down the backroads of Lee County, deep in the heart of the Black Belt South with Willie Ricks, my first mentor and SNCC supervisor. In a couple of years, he would be the very first one to issue the call for "Black Power," along with Stokely Carmichael, during the March Against Fear in rural Mississippi. The Black Belt was an unbroken chain of Black majority–populated counties stretching from Virginia to East Texas. I was rolling into Lee County, which had the despicable distinction, I was told, of being the county with the highest number of lynchings in the United States. With Leesburg as its county seat, I was in a rural farming stretch of earth nestled between two hotbeds of the movement: Albany, in Dougherty County, to the south; and Americus, in Sumter County, to the north.

Lee County was far from being in a lull, though, as the SNCC, through Willie's efforts, was building a formidable presence there. In fact, three Black churches, where Willie had won support and was holding mass meetings and political education classes, had been torched, burned to the ground as direct warning signals from area Klansman and white leadership. Yet these Black citizens, members of those very churches, were stepping up their intensity.

As the school bus continued its orchestrated tumble along the red clay road, I tried to catch my breath. Less than a year ago, I was in high school, an instructor colonel in the NDCC (the National Defense Cadet Corps), and now I was a rookie field secretary with the SNCC. There was no turning back. Perhaps it was the steady bouncing about in the seat of the bus, but my mind began to reflect on a childhood experience that taught me one of the most important lessons of my life.

•

By the time I was eight, I had graduated from being the reluctant, homesick participant at his very first YMCA summer camp in Lancaster, Texas—a kid who wrote a one-line postcard to his mom saying, "Dear Mom, I want to come home vary [sic] soon!"—to becoming a pro at camping. In fact, I was ready for an even bigger adventure: riding a horse, alone and unaided, along the camp trails.

When the big day arrived, one of our camp counselors saddled the horses and helped me and the other campers mount them, then led us around the campground. The counselor in charge of the horses was known by all of us simply as "Red." Little did we know that Red, our faithful camp counselor, would soon become quite famous in our local sports scene as a professional wrestler. We could watch some of his matches live on television—which was a really big deal in the mid-'50s. We had only had two or three channels then and very few shows. So to have a live, daytime television show featuring a Black man as an action-hero figure was miraculous indeed. But by then, Red had already proven to be my real-life hero that fateful summer.

This was my first day as a rider, and I was to ride a large horse (which I later learned was a quarter horse). Our first basic lesson was to grab the reins and to pull them in the direction you wanted to go. If you pulled the reins left, the horse would go left, and if you pulled the reins right, the horse would know to go right. Evidently, I wanted to go backward, as once I mounted the horse, I pulled his reins straight back and continued to do so. The message to the horse must have been to stand up on his hind legs—and so he did! I went tumbling down to the ground. The horse continued to rise and fall, kicking his front legs and eventually prancing about, planting one of his hooves on my head and face several times.

In true hero fashion, Red quickly came over and gained control of the horse, then picked me up with one arm, slinging me over his shoulder. He hopped back on his horse and hurried off to the infirmary. By the time we reached the first aid station, Red's T-shirt was no longer a pristine white, but soaked in my bright red blood.

Despite all that blood, I am not sure if I was anything more than dazed. I never lost consciousness, and it was soon determined that I wasn't seriously hurt. More than anything, I felt scared and embarrassed by it all. I trembled for several moments and wondered what had just happened. Red came to visit me later that day and asked how I felt. I did not give him an answer, but he somehow got my message: my horse-riding days were over! He calmly looked me in the eyes and told me that tomorrow I "must get back on that same horse and ride again."

I looked at him like he was a mad dog, wondering how anyone in his right mind, especially an eyewitness to the fiasco, could make a statement like that. In my mind, it was simple: the horse threw me off and that was that. "I ain't no cowboy and I ain't ever riding ever again!" Red calmly and confidently said that if I let this incident dominate me, then I would most likely treat other battles and other blows the same way. From here on out, I would never really overcome hard or seemingly devastating situations. I do not recall his exact words, but his look, his sincerity, and his message—to get back on that horse and ride him again—was what I needed. His advice was the best and perhaps the only response to that situation.

The next day, he and the horse were waiting for me. I slowly approached the horse, ready to take off running if he displayed *any* hostility or a hint of gruffness toward me. But there were no signs of orneriness. It was just being a horse—standing there, nibbling grass, in his own world. Not concerned with me at all. I patted the horse's head, rubbed his neck, and then grabbed the reins and carefully got on. The horse offered no resistance, no shudders or tension. I moved slowly, deliberately, placing my feet in the raised stirrups, and then rode off slowly. Red rode up front, leading the small group of ponies and horses mounted by other campers. He kept looking back at me and smiling. After a while, I slowly began to find a sense of calm and ease. By the end of the ride, I felt like I was a cowboy again.

Red's advice would serve me well for decades to come, particularly

uring my pending movement days when I would literally be thrown or knocked down repeatedly and by forces much greater than that quarter horse.

•

For a long time, especially during my early days with the SNCC and the movement, I felt invincible. Even in the constant face of fear and death around me. Around us. I was still so young and coming into my own.

Surprisingly, I became a very good driver during this time, mainly out of necessity on the highways and back roads of the Black Belt South. One had to be prepared to flee at virtually any moment, from either a pickup truck loaded with white men with rifle racks, or a county sheriff who was out to have some fun "harassing niggers," or "outside agitators," as we were often referred to by the local rednecks. I learned by practice to drive at night without headlights on over unpaved country roads, traveling at high speeds from pursuing Klansmen or local police. I had to do so at least three times throughout my tour of duty with the SNCC in Georgia, with Willie by my side.

Eventually, SNCC was awarded a fleet of new '65 Plymouth Furies. In a way, they became the official auto of SNCC workers. We went virtually overnight from jalopies and hand-me-down used cars to late-model speedsters, all equipped with CB radios. The CB radios allowed us to be in constant contact with one another.

But this 180-degree turnaround with SNCC vehicles came about at an immeasurable human expense, the result of horrible losses: the murders of James Chaney, Andrew Goodwin, and Michael Schwerner in Philadelphia, Mississippi, during the Mississippi Freedom Summer Project of 1964. With their deaths at the hands of a Klan/police death squad came a great public outcry resounding around the world. Massive waves of support poured in for civil rights workers in the Deep South. A lot of money came toward SNCC from the Jewish community for safety to rekindle their fellowship. I saw no harm in her leaving me, thinking a short visit was the best thing all around. I would not see Bettie again until ten months later, in Selma, where I was shocked to be introduced to her baby and my beautiful daughter, Angela. Her birth would be one of the most precious gifts received during the struggle.

My first solo assignment as a SNCC field secretary took me back to Thomasville, Georgia, which is located just north of the Florida state line deep in Southwest Georgia. There I met Hiram Thompson, who became my key link to the community. He quickly became my closest confidant, one I considered a brother in the struggle. Through Hiram, I was able to forge strong bonds with well-respected community leaders like the Reverend Doctor I. L. Mullins, pastor of the First Baptist Church and president of the local NAACP chapter. Rev. Mullins allowed SNCC to host mass meetings at his church.

Hiram was a thirty-three-degree mason, a leader in the meat cutter's union, and a well-respected member of the Elks Lodge, among other deep ties. Through our kinship, I not only became quickly accepted and rapidly immersed in Thomasville's Black community, but also an honorary member of the Thompson family. My life in Thomasville and my work with the voter registration drives largely grew through the Thompson family's care and support. Their home was located just a few blocks from the SNCC safe house. His relatives—especially his mother and sisters, as well as his fiancée (and subsequent wife) Judy—provided me with a home away from home and a sense of belonging. Through their circle of influence and connections, I soon found myself in the loop on all the ins and outs of the community.

But my connection to the Thompsons ran deeper than that. There was Sandra.

My relationship with Hiram's sister Sandra grew over several years. She was a young woman with a radiant smile, attractive and friendly, and I felt relaxed and comfortable around her. But I kept my emerging feelings about her to myself and played the field, deciding to be open and intended to derail the assembly of citizens seeking to register to vote. These recruits mostly wore white helmets and khakis, carried billy clubs and often electric cattle prodders that would be used for "crowd control." Bettie would roll down her window and shout obscenities at them, calling them "crackers" and every demeaning word possible, and daring them to do something about it. I tried to restrain her, pull her back and put my hand over her mouth, but without much success—she'd squirm and break free again and again. It would take a word from Silas—"Hush up, Bettie"—to get her to calm down and be quiet. Bettie was a routine participant in the everyday struggle during the Selma campaign, assisting in the office making posters, calling folk and passing leaflets during the day, and singing in the mass rallies at the Brown Chapel AME Church in the evenings. We became a pair during those few weeks I was there.

She eventually left Selma and we lived together in Thomasville, Georgia, for several months with her classmate Gwen Smith and her husband Reverend Tom Brown, who was also her best friend and a SNCC field secretary in Selma. We'd work together in Thomasville, organizing around voter registration, holding mass meetings. Some weekend nights we'd travel to visit clubs in town or as far away as Tallahassee. Tom, acting as her manager, would mysteriously persuade club owners or band leaders to call on Bettie to sing the blues. She became a local hit. By August, we traveled to the Democratic National Convention in Atlantic City to join in solidarity with the seating of the Mississippi Freedom Democratic Party, recognized as official delegates. In Atlantic City, we marched, sat in, sang, prayed, and lobbied on the boardwalk for nearly a week. When the convention concluded, we were left with a bitter taste, as a "compromise" was reached to save face for the Democratic Party and LBJ, one that proved to be a slap in the face of all freedom lovers, as the delegates were not seated.

We decided it was time to return to our local battlefields to continue the fight for equal and fair representation. Bettie, however, said she would head north to Washington, D.C., to stay with friends who wanted listened to each other's side of the story. Everyone was given the opportunity to argue for his or her beliefs and values. This brought beauty to the struggle. As did the eventual shared organizing efforts of SNCC workers with dynamic locals, like Fannie Lou Hamer. This established reciprocity between SNCC and the communities we served, allowing all to learn from each other, thus empowering our shared efforts.

•

My first tour of duty in the Deep South spanned three years—from 1964 to 1967. During this time, I met and worked alongside people who became lifelong friends and comrades. One would even become the mother of my first child.

I met Bettie Mae Fikes in 1964, while she was screaming at white deputies in her hometown of Selma, Alabama, as they were being deputized to beat and harass its Black citizens. She was an inside agitator, whose audacity both scared and uplifted me. Bettie was a member of the SNCC Freedom Singers and deemed "the voice of Selma." The first time I heard her sing "This Little Light of Mine," I knew she was special. When she sang in a packed church for a mass rally—her voice rising and falling through the chorus, piercing the shell around our hearts, uniting our spirits as one, daring us to struggle, daring us to win—I felt I knew her, had to know more. We began to sit and talk inside the SNCC office and a little later we'd walk and talk. She was a true militant, unafraid and audacious almost to the extreme. On one occasion Bettie and I were in the backseat of the SNCC vehicle driven by Silas Norman, the SNCC project manager, surveying the streets near the courthouse on reconnaissance late one evening. We were looking for the best pathways to and from the church so those participants on "Freedom Day" could travel with the least police/vigilante obstructions. Police chief Jim Clark and Selma's white powers that be deputized and organized every white male over the age of twenty-one as auxiliary support for the police's extralegal methods improvements. Beginning in late '64, throughout Mississippi there existed a network of SNCC base stations ("Freedom Houses"), each equipped with CB transmitters where one could be confident of constant contact radio linkages. The money also allowed SNCC to equip itself with decent cars to carry out the work of organizing communities, registering new voters, and educating a people.

Not all SNCC workers were allotted the new Furies or were equipped with CB radios. A good number used their own cars. But even those with new cars or CBs were not assured of absolute protection; a better chance to even the odds, but no guarantees. We would learn we'd need every chance we could get.

In 1965, one of my dearest comrades, George Bess—a SNCC field secretary from Tallahassee, Georgia, and a former student activist at Florida A&M University—was killed on a Mississippi highway one night. He drove his own vehicle and had no CB radio, and hence no way to contact anyone as he was chased down by right-wing, racist, vigilante night troopers. His car was forced off the road, landing upside down in a riverbed. He—being trapped inside—drowned.

Such tragedies did not deter others or me but rather strengthened our resolve to keep working and fighting for justice. So many of us found ourselves called to the struggle in a similar way, having dropped out of school to join the movement. We were in this war together and many of us—particularly the field secretaries—considered ourselves to be family.

I was moved by the culture of SNCC, in its effort to build a sense of community and equality among all the workers. For example, all Freedom Houses were equipped with a pantry stocked with food donated from all over the country. All labels were removed from every can, and you had to eat whatever you opened. This counteracted ego and favoritism and evened the playing field.

Even in our meetings, there was a sense of a utopian democracy within the organization. We would meet as long as it took, until we came to a consensus. We tried to resolve as much as we could and intentionally during my pending movement days when I would literally be thrown or knocked down repeatedly and by forces much greater than that quarter horse.

•

For a long time, especially during my early days with the SNCC and the movement, I felt invincible. Even in the constant face of fear and death around me. Around us. I was still so young and coming into my own.

Surprisingly, I became a very good driver during this time, mainly out of necessity on the highways and back roads of the Black Belt South. One had to be prepared to flee at virtually any moment, from either a pickup truck loaded with white men with rifle racks, or a county sheriff who was out to have some fun "harassing niggers," or "outside agitators," as we were often referred to by the local rednecks. I learned by practice to drive at night without headlights on over unpaved country roads, traveling at high speeds from pursuing Klansmen or local police. I had to do so at least three times throughout my tour of duty with the SNCC in Georgia, with Willie by my side.

Eventually, SNCC was awarded a fleet of new '65 Plymouth Furies. In a way, they became the official auto of SNCC workers. We went virtually overnight from jalopies and hand-me-down used cars to late-model speedsters, all equipped with CB radios. The CB radios allowed us to be in constant contact with one another.

But this 180-degree turnaround with SNCC vehicles came about at an immeasurable human expense, the result of horrible losses: the murders of James Chaney, Andrew Goodwin, and Michael Schwerner in Philadelphia, Mississippi, during the Mississippi Freedom Summer Project of 1964. With their deaths at the hands of a Klan/police death squad came a great public outcry resounding around the world. Massive waves of support poured in for civil rights workers in the Deep South. A lot of money came toward SNCC from the Jewish community for safety

Despite all that blood, I am not sure if I was anything more than dazed. I never lost consciousness, and it was soon determined that I wasn't seriously hurt. More than anything, I felt scared and embarrassed by it all. I trembled for several moments and wondered what had just happened. Red came to visit me later that day and asked how I felt. I did not give him an answer, but he somehow got my message: my horse-riding days were over! He calmly looked me in the eyes and told me that tomorrow I "must get back on that same horse and ride again."

I looked at him like he was a mad dog, wondering how anyone in his right mind, especially an eyewitness to the fiasco, could make a statement like that. In my mind, it was simple: the horse threw me off and that was that. "I ain't no cowboy and I ain't ever riding ever again!" Red calmly and confidently said that if I let this incident dominate me, then I would most likely treat other battles and other blows the same way. From here on out, I would never really overcome hard or seemingly devastating situations. I do not recall his exact words, but his look, his sincerity, and his message—to get back on that horse and ride him again—was what I needed. His advice was the best and perhaps the only response to that situation.

The next day, he and the horse were waiting for me. I slowly approached the horse, ready to take off running if he displayed *any* hostility or a hint of gruffness toward me. But there were no signs of orneriness. It was just being a horse—standing there, nibbling grass, in his own world. Not concerned with me at all. I patted the horse's head, rubbed his neck, and then grabbed the reins and carefully got on. The horse offered no resistance, no shudders or tension. I moved slowly, deliberately, placing my feet in the raised stirrups, and then rode off slowly. Red rode up front, leading the small group of ponies and horses mounted by other campers. He kept looking back at me and smiling. After a while, I slowly began to find a sense of calm and ease. By the end of the ride, I felt like I was a cowboy again.

Red's advice would serve me well for decades to come, particularly free. When I first showed up in Thomasville, there were several local girls interested in me, drawn to know this new guy, the stranger in town. Community organizing—and voter registration work in particular—welcomes every opportunity to make friends and build ties. So, I indulged in them.

Moreover, Sandra was overcoming the loss of her longtime boyfriend. One evening, as we sat alone on her front porch, she calmly revealed that just a year earlier she watched her boyfriend struggle repeatedly with depression, turning to alcohol to deaden the demon voices in his head. One night, while they sat talking in his car on a deserted path along the local lovers' lane, he calmly got out and walked to the front as she sat inside. He then pulled a pistol from his pants pocket, shot himself in the head, and fell dead. I had no words. I could not even form a question. All I could do was hold her and feel her breathe.

From that intimate moment of trust, we eventually blossomed into more than friends and supported each other throughout my times in Thomasville and beyond.

I had the opportunity to work with a fellow Dallas native and fellow Booker T. Washington High School graduate during this time as well. Roy Shields was project manager for the Southwest Georgia project in 1964–65. SNCC was racially inclusive then and thus we had white people working in the office. One of them edited a statement Roy had written, provoking his ire because the man had changed it without his permission. Roy responded with fists to the man's head and face, followed by a toss down the stairs! For some time, SNCC's leadership had debated whether to become a Black organization exclusively. SNCC built Freedom Schools to combat the third-class "sharecropper education" that prevailed throughout the South. While whites worked alongside us, we did not want to perpetuate a sense of superiority with their presence, as the damage caused by the image of "smart white teachers" elevating "ignorant Black people" became obvious.

In 1966, SNCC became Black-only. We encouraged those

sympathetic whites to go home and work in their own communities to fight against racism. Around this time, James Meredith was shot during his noble March Against Fear. This attack sparked more local involvement and led to the evolution of the Black Power Movement. We were growing tired of so many deaths and beatings and were ready to fight for our destiny. The right to define our own selves calls for power. There was always an element of resistance within SNCC, against "color blindness" and the exclusion of the wealth of Black Heritage. We were not foolish. We were also not wedded to the philosophy of non-violent pacification; like the Deacons of Self Defense, the young men and women of SNCC were not without arms to protect themselves.

We were maturing personally and as a mighty movement, even beyond the southern struggle. A position paper was written in 1967 for the people of Palestine, condemning Israel and Zionist practices for colonial invasions and genocide. SNCC took a stand for the Palestinian people, drafted by Jim Farmer, Executive Secretary of SNCC—and then the money abruptly stopped coming from the Jewish community. This was a major teachable moment for the organization, and it did not deter our stance or quiet our call for local and global human rights, for the right of self-determination for all people.

By '67, it was time for SNCC to expand its reach. In a few months, I would find myself back in Dallas to establish one of SNCC's newest chapters. This effort would prove to be the beginning of my maturation into leading a fight for dignity, power, and self-determination in my hometown. Life had brought me home and near full circle, except now I was not the same person who had boarded a train to Georgia to attend Morehouse College. I had become a teacher, facilitator, and radical and I was back in my own backyard.

CHAPTER SIX

I HITCHHIKED FROM DALLAS TO HOUSTON one hot summer day in 1967 for a pre-arranged visit with Lee Otis Johnson, the Houston SNCC Chairman. I was not sure of the scope of responsibilities, organizational challenges, or heartaches that came with the territory of leading Dallas' newly formed SNCC chapter, especially given it was in an urban setting, and wanted to glean as much as I could from him.

Lee Otis quickly became my mentor. He invited me to his home, which also served as his office. It was an apartment in the Black neighborhood of Fifth Ward, just off Houston's Eastex Freeway. He spoke almost nonstop from the moment I arrived that afternoon through the dawn hours the following day.

The next morning, he shook me awake with a gruff voice and a stern look on his face. He handed me the telephone receiver saying, "See, this is what these motherfuckers do. This is what you will go through." I held the receiver to my ear and heard my own voice saying the exact words I said the day before in a conversation with Lee Otis's lawyer, Bobby Caldwell, who was also in Houston.

I was amazed. This marked my first of many unmistakeable confirmations of police surveillance. Johnson believed the playback was no accident, rather an attempt for the "pigs" to let us know that we were being watched and that nothing we did escaped them.

Following my stints in Selma and Mississippi, and well after my return home to Dallas, I received a phone call from Sandra informing me that Hiram had been locked up for his labor organizing work at the Sunnyland meatpacking plant. He was being falsely accused of making violent threats to those opposed to the union organizing in the plant. She wanted to know if I could return, help support him before and during his trial. I dropped everything and drove to Thomasville, arriving a day before the trial.

I stayed with the family. Sandra was now married to a man everyone called "Brother." He was the foreman of a crew of day laborers, who were paid six dollars a day to work in the fields. Although San was married, we held a special bond, one that made me a rival of sorts in Brother's eyes. His body language reflected his uneasiness whenever the three of us were in the same room. Sometimes, he would snort or leave the room. San would deflect his resentment. One day, following the trial, the tension exploded into a drunken, public tussle between me and Brother.

While Hiram expressed confidence in the case, he was aware that fairness does not always apply to Black people, especially those who want to challenge the status quo, organize unions, and "rouse up discontent through agitation," as the local daily newspapers' editorial would put it. Hiram was one of four men tried in this case. I was introduced to their lawyer, who seemed very detached. I armed myself with a yellow legal pad, a pen behind my ear, and several questions for the lawyer. During the trial, I sat in the row of seats behind the defense team's table with the family, San at my side.

To my disbelief, after the opening statements and just hours after lunch, the prosecution wrapped up their side and rested their case. I hurriedly scanned through my notes, page by scribbled page, and it struck me that, yes, in every single charge raised, in every witness's account of the threats, intimidating actions, and physical encounters, Hiram's name was never mentioned, not even once. While the courtroom was adjourned, I hurried over to the defense table and told Hiram and the lawyer that the prosecution had no case. There was absolutely no evidence pointing to Hiram.

Once the trial reconvened, the defense lawyer stated there was factual evidence that needed to be reviewed. He asked for a pause in the action and received a timeout from the judge. He looked over his notes, walked over to the court reporter, and came back to the table with a determined look on his brow. He asked for and was astonishingly granted the right to exclude Hiram from all charges. My dear friend was released then and there.

I stayed on for a few more days, celebrating Hiram's release and witnessing the remaining trial. Sandra and her husband were not getting on well. He drank a lot and they argued back and forth about issues unknown to me. Her husband never grew violent with her, for she would, without one doubt, kick his ass and his entire body to the curb.

•

Shortly after the murder of Dr. King, everything around us, near and far, ramped up to another level of intensity. New handwriting was on the wall: there was increased urgency to act, to move, to contest the status quo of oppression, injustices, and racism. The movement kicked up another notch, and people who had previously sat on the fence were now jumping off and over to a more militant, less appeasing stance.

One such person was Donald Ray Williams. His once-latent consciousness spurred sharply into action, as he broke from his daily lifestyle and leapt heart-first into the growing movement. While he was riding the bus home from a day's work as a grocery-store butcher one hot summer afternoon in 1968, Donald Ray's bus stopped adjacent to a picket line organized by SNCC, protesting the policies and behaviors of the OK Supermarket chain in Dallas. OK was a white-owned enterprise of eleven convenience stores, and ten of those stores were concentrated within inner-city neighborhoods.

Donald Ray saw and heard Black youth marching in front of the store at the corner of Pine Street and Oakland Avenue in South Dallas. His near-dozing eyes were blitzed by the sight of a throng of Black men and women carrying signs that read *Don't Shop Here!* and shouting, with raised fists, *OK Supermarket Ain't OK!* He was immediately roused, and without second thoughts bounded off the bus, drawn by those sights and sounds.

Within a month of that day, Donald Ray was no longer a butcher, having quit the job to become a full-time organizer with Dallas SNCC in the West Dallas community, as well as a journalist with the *Black Disciple* newsletter, where he was the author of one of its regular columns, "Notes from Vietnam." He was also no longer Donald Ray, but Kwesi Williams (Kwesi being an Ashanti name for males born on Sunday) and one of my closest comrades. In no time, he became an effective speaker and agitator for Black power.

The summer of 1968 was unlike any other and hotter than the devil's armpits. These were times when irresistible forces repeatedly faced immovable objects. These were the brutally hot days and beastly cold nights when more and more people—those for the right and the power of self-determination and those for the love of human rights and justice— arose to fight. They demanded it and pursued it in tried and proven fashions, in addition to bold, emerging, new ways.

This wave of humanity faced off, toe to toe, against those who despised change and who had an array of seemingly unlimited material resources to impose their oppressive will. These were well-armed, well-financed, deeply entrenched palaces of power, kingdoms duty bound to crush the movement. They pledged to do so wholly, legally, by force, and through deceitfully cunning and devastating machinery designed to erase the future and the past of this upsurge, attacking even its memory, preventing even the slightest notion of its rising again from ever taking hold again.

At the time, those of us who were already active in the fight for liberation were being viewed as having newly discovered or rediscovered value. SNCC's ranks were growing exponentially, and, so, too, was the demand for our understanding, our perspectives, our presence.

One call for our input came from Black students at East Texas State University (now Texas A&M University-Commerce). There, a newly founded group called the African American Student Society at East Texas (ASSET) was on the move. They carried out a march against the university's narrow and bankrupt racist policies. University administrators threatened them with disciplinary actions while crowds of white students gathered to jeer and hiss. The potential for expulsions, arrests, and violence mounted all because they were speaking up about their plight and calling for an end to racist practices.

The ASSET students turned to Dallas SNCC and invited us to campus to discuss how we could support them with ideas and actions. We arrived late one evening. They'd arranged a rally with most of the black students present. We heard their concerns and advised them to keep the efforts going, and, in fact, to step up their campaign. It was a call and response exchange that grew in intensity. By the end of the dialogue, their resolve was reinforced, the cause reaffirmed, and we closed on a high note. The atmosphere transformed into one of celebration with raised fists, high-fives, laughs, and music.

One-on-one conversation began and I started to talk with Felicia Johnson, a freshman from the Oak Cliff community of Dallas, who was very serious, and a core leader within ASSET's ranks. We connected that night and spent time alone. I learned that night that although the campus activities were her very first involvement in the struggle, she was not afraid. She expressed some leeriness about some of the tactical courses of the student leadership. She felt that the administration was not going to listen to their demands unless they exerted more pressure through stronger, more direct actions.

When she returned home for the summer, the Dallas SNCC chapter was immersed in many actions. She joined us, participating fully in our boycott of OK Supermarket, the chain of ghetto-gouging stores in

South Dallas. By the end of summer, I was charged with a felony for our actions ("malicious destruction of private property over the value of $50") and held in the Dallas County Jail on a $10,000 bond along with my SNCC comrade Matthew Johnson (named as co-conspirator). Felicia joined the community campaign to free us and did not return to school for her college studies, much to the great disappointment of her dad, who felt she was making the biggest mistake of her young life.

While I was locked up, a rumor circulated that there would be an attempt to hurt or kill me. When that information reached my mother's ears, she initiated a telephone campaign, flooding the jail system with calls to "not mess with Ernie." I had been isolated, first held in solitary confinement, where I refused food for the first ten days I remained there. Later, I was removed and housed in a remote area of the jail. I was the lone prisoner in an emptied ten-cell tank. One night, Sheriff Bill Decker came to my wing and called me over to the bars to tell me that people were wearing out his phone lines, saying that nothing bad had better happen to me. He scoffed, saying, "Boy, I knew your grandpa, and I can guarantee you ain't nothing gonna happen to you in this jail."

A "Free Ernie" campaign was launched. Money for bond was being raised via a multitude of approaches and resources. Rallies were held and *Free Ernie* T-shirts sold. Prominent citizens and community leaders including Dr. Emmett Conrad, Dr. Marion Brooks, and Rev. Willliam Farmer put up their properties to insure my freedom. I had no idea of the depth and breadth of those efforts until I was finally released. When the sum of money was raised to free one of us, Matthew said it had to be him since he had a wife and children and he felt on the verge of committing suicide if he stayed in any longer. He had even fashioned a noose made of shoelaces and cloth. I was relieved that he was able to get out.

I was in indescribable awe of the whole-scale dedication and multiple sacrifices made by so many family members, friends, and strangers, and I felt especially grateful to Felicia. When I was released on bond, I knew that I had found a woman with whom I could spend my life. I asked her to marry me. On November 19, 1968, one month after my release, we were married in the living room of her family home, decked in African attire.

CHAPTER SEVEN

DURING THIS TIME, WE ACTIVISTS often relied more on spontaneity and the actions dictated by the moment-to-moment experiences than any theory or formulas. We were in new territories, undergoing a sharp break with our pasts, and treading in piranha-infested waters. One evening, a few of us gathered in a South Dallas lounge, listening to the sounds from a jukebox and testing lessons and arguments gleaned from our community canvasses. In hindsight, this practice was our own version of a classroom, creating verbal and attitudinal responses through a collective rehashing of the day's events. We were interrupted by someone coming into the bar saying that the cops were outside arresting a youngster for shoplifting at a neighboring convenience store in the same strip mall.

Nothing more needed to be said. We were there in an instant. Some went to "inquire" with the police in loud, irritated voices, while others questioned the store owner. The kid, a seven- or eight-year-old Black boy, was in tears. He stood, sandwiched between two cops who were asking his name, address, and the whereabouts of his parents. Someone recognized the child and described the location of his house so his mother could be notified of unfolding events. The police seemed determined to take the kid to jail or the juvenile home, for stealing and possibly being on the late-night streets, unsupervised.

We were offering a way out for the child to the non-Black store owner, stating we would pay for the cookies or candies the boy supposedly stole. The store owner was unmoved, however, and the police began to handcuff the boy and place him in the squad car. By that time, someone said the boy's mother was on her way, but the police were in no mood to wait around, especially with the heat we were generating, and justified their stance by saying a crime had been committed and this was "police business."

One police officer noticed his patrol car had four flat tires. He became alarmed and got on his radio to seek help. A crowd was now building outside the store, and we shifted to teaching mode. We SNCC members seized this as an opportunity to raise consciousness.

"Look at these pigs!" one of us implored the curious crowd. "These cops want to arrest this little boy for some candy!"

"We can pay for the candy!" someone yelled, and others followed suit, shouting, "You've got the candy back, honky!" Murmurs and grumblings began to swell within the growing crowd.

"Why do these motherfuckers want to lock him up?" someone asked.

"Don't they have anything better to do?" another said.

By that time, another patrol car pulled up and the officer in that car joined the other cops. They huddled up, trying to figure a way out. The newly arrived officer got on his radio to call for more help. A wrecker truck arrived, and while its driver attended to the first car's flat tires, someone pointed out that the second patrol car's tires were now flat. Two other police cars arrived. The crowd was getting larger and more boisterous.

The lights on the second car were flashing and the cops took on a more defensive stance. One placed the boy in the first patrol car. Finally, a woman arrived claiming to be his mother and demanded to see her son. The police told her that they were charging him with a crime and that she would need to go downtown to get him. Two other cars arrived while we were still in our educating mode among our neighbors.

We began to call out to all that if this store were ours, this never would have happened. "Look at these pigs hassling and oppressing a kid, when the real crooks and criminals roam free to do their crimes," someone shouted. We reminded onlookers that our people know how to treat each other with respect, but the outsiders who owned our land and controlled our economies were in South Dallas only to take our money and run.

The gathering had bloomed into a full community rally. More squad cars arrived; another police wrecker pulled up. It was even taking on a comical tone as the keystones on site were way out of their league. Given the circumstances, they were required to stay and had no choice but to be the subject of the day's "lesson" in our makeshift, spur-of-the-moment classroom. Although only ten minutes may have elapsed, it seemed that each second was a blow against the establishment.

Suddenly, someone in the crowd called out, announcing with notes of surprise and glee, that there were now *four* police cars on flats. We had no idea which member of the crowd was responsible for the flat tires, showing tremendous initiative without any prompting from any of their "teachers." School was in session and the boy was finally released into his mother's custody.

•

Through 1967 and beyond, we felt it. Witnessed it. First, as whispers, curious coincidences, accidents, stings and blows, that then dramatically morphed into an unfolding pattern of naked raids with guns drawn on households, paid informants, agent provocateurs lurking near and far, senseless arrests, the pilfering of our trash cans, and varying degrees of nonsensical charges and complaints.

Late one night as he drove home, Kwesi was pulled over by Dallas police for no apparent reason. The officers asked for his ID, questioned him, and then presented Kwesi with a matchbox of weed supposedly found on the ground near his car, stating, "This is yours." Despite his protests and his having nothing to do with the drug, he was pulled from his car, handcuffed, taken to jail, and charged with possession of marijuana.

It was a serious offense, one that was used to sentence my friend and mentor Lee Otis Johnson to thirty years imprisonment a year earlier, and one used four years later to sentence Stoney Burns, the editor of Dallas' very popular and radical weekly magazine *Notes from the Underground*, to ten years and one day. (The one day was added to insure he would not be eligible for parole!) The charge Kwesi faced carried a one-year to life imprisonment term.

Encounters between Dallas SNCC and the police had become a routine and escalated to a boiling point. Once I even received a speeding ticket from a Dallas police officer before ever entering my car. The cop had been sitting in his cruiser, parked in front of my apartment on South Boulevard in South Dallas, for at least an hour. As I walked out of my apartment, he got out and approached me with a speeding citation in hand. He presented me with the ticket saying he "thought I'd never come out" and that his shift was nearly over and he "could no longer wait to follow me" and ticket me later.

On another occasion, I remember being stopped and interrogated by an officer who claimed to be a member of the Dallas police's intelligence unit. He declared that he had films of me from a party I held at my apartment revealing "freaky sex acts." In addition, I was once given a copy of a free weekly community "newspaper" that was more of an ad page for nightclubs and liquor stores. It featured a collage of "neighborhood scenes" that included a photo of me and other SNCC members in front of our Oakland Avenue offices. A stealth photographer, someone secretly using a telephoto lens from a parked vehicle, had obviously shot it.

One of the most brazen acts of harassment and intimidation by the police took place one evening when a caravan of four or five SNCC cars—traveling to my mother's house for a home-cooked meal—was followed by at least one dozen police cars and motorcycles all the way to her doorstep.

On July 4, 1968, several SNCC members, including me, were standing at the corner of Atlanta Street and Forest Avenue in South Dallas when suddenly several police squad cars swooped in, with officers jumping out, guns drawn, barking orders for all of us to freeze. We were told to put our hands up and were patted down. When nothing incriminating was discovered, they returned to their cars without explanation and drove off. Later, trying to make some sense of the episode, we reminded ourselves about a recent conversation we had in which someone, in jest or with bravado, or perhaps just as a fleeting thought, said it would be more fitting to riot than have a picnic on the Fourth of July—a more appropriate act of protest of America's hypocrisy of claiming to be the home to freedom and independence. These acts reflected the depth of surveillance we more than suspected. Someone out there was taking us very seriously, looking for an excuse to bust us or put us in a grave.

During a meeting at the home of Wade Chambers, a professor at Southern Methodist University and sponsor of the Students for a Democratic Society chapter on campus, someone noticed two people in the yard with a boom microphone trying to record us. There were about thirty to fifty people in attendance. It seemed as if cops and their cronies followed us with obvious intent to be seen. We opened the door shouting at them until they scurried away.

•

The dangers were real. To counter police intimidation, we Dallas SNCC members started our own police patrol, took pictures, and carried guns.

We had home bases in West Dallas, South Dallas, and in Oak Cliff. Our West Dallas site was in the projects at Ruth Jefferson's house. Ms. Jefferson virtually overnight became the leader of the local welfare rights organization, and one of the strongest allies of Dallas SNCC. She changed her hair overnight from straight to an afro during our three-day sit-in protest at the county welfare offices! Her entire pathway, her life's journey, was transformed anew through those days and nights sitting in protest at the welfare office. One night, during our patrol in West Dallas, members discovered a uniformed cop crawling around her apartment. He wore no badge or headgear. He backed away with his hands up after Eddie clanked a round in his shotgun and pointed it at him.

These were hot and tense times. It felt like we were in a crucible. We were being followed, intimidated, harassed, and arrested regularly. We were infiltrated by undercover folks and paid informants, from apartment managers and security guards to secret moles within our own ranks.

We often passed out flyers and spoke to customers gathered at Good Luck, a popular local hamburger joint, to eat and socialize. At one gathering, a security guard approached us and tried to run us off the premises. Later, we learned he filed a peace bond on me for talking back to him and accused other SNCC members of "threatening his life" and cursing him out. A hearing was held in Judge Richburg's court. Richburg was notorious for cruel sentences. Approximately one hundred people showed up to our hearing, at which an owner of one of the OK Supermarkets interrupted to accuse us of tearing up his store.

With all this going on, I felt obligated to buy a rifle, especially after being charged with the OK Supermarket property destruction and draft evasion.

On that fateful morning in 1969 the police raided all three Dallas SNCC community headquarters. They even put guns to the heads of John Woods' and Jackie Harris' kids in West Dallas. They made a show of the thirteen guns they confiscated from all three locations to prove we were revolutionaries. Many of our guns were purchased legally. When raiding my house on Cedar Crest, they sealed off the street, had deputy sheriffs from the county, state troopers, and agents from the FBI and ATF. SNCC members were officially public enemy number one in Dallas.

CHAPTER EIGHT

BY JUNE 1969, I HAD racked up three felony cases: two federal charges and one state conviction. The federal cases I was to stand trial for were violation of the Selective Service Act (commonly referred to as "draft evading") and a federal firearms violation for legally purchasing a thirty-caliber carbine rifle from a Medallion store (now a Target) while out on an appeal bond. At the time, I was actively challenging the ten-year conviction for "destruction of private property, over the value of $50" in the OK Supermarkets case through the higher courts.

While awaiting trial for the federal charges, and as a condition for obtaining release on bond, I was stripped of my passport and placed on travel restrictions, unable to venture outside of the US District Court for the Northern District of Texas' jurisdiction without written permission. Since I could not afford an attorney, I was handed one who previously specialized in tax law and had no criminal trial expertise to be my legal representative. I was, however, able to travel for the next several months outside of the Northern District as well as outside the state of Texas. I submitted requested travel dates, the purpose of my travels, and the addresses and contact information of my destinations to the US Attorney through the court-appointed lawyer. For months, this process successfully worked each time my request to travel was submitted.

Nearly all my travel was associated with speaking engagements at universities or at conferences. I followed strict protocol during this critical time, traveling to Pennsylvania, Georgia, and Ohio to speak. Due to the increasing attacks, threats, and false arrests made upon SNCC members, we implemented a policy that none of us travel alone, that we always be accompanied by another SNCC staffer to mitigate opportunities by police to harass or place trumped-up charges, as had happened to Kwesi and others.

In June 1969, I was invited to speak at the World Council of Churches in Greenwich, Connecticut. Leading up to my scheduled departure date, I communicated back and forth with my lawyer, inquiring as to whether my trip had been approved. And each time, my attorney would say that he had submitted the request and expected a response "any moment." But none ever materialized.

A couple of days prior to the departure, my attorney began making excuses, saying the federal prosecutor was busy, tied up in other cases and proceedings, but "not to worry." He was sure approval would be granted, as it had in each previous instance. Less than twelve hours before departure time, I finally received a call from the attorney saying that although there had still been no official word, he felt it "safe to travel" and that "they're sure to approve," as they had always done before. So, I went to the airport as planned.

At Love Field, I paced nervously at the gate because Kwesi, who was assigned to join me on this trip, had not shown up. The flight had been delayed for some reason, but it appeared that all the passengers had boarded the plane except me and Kwesi. I bit my nails, marching back and forth near the entry ramp, hoping he would show up. There were men wearing suits and dark shades milling around the gate, men I innocently assumed were there for another flight or some other business. The truth about the unexplained flight delay and their presence would become unmistakably clear a few hours later. More than fifteen minutes past our scheduled departure time, with the plane still parked at the gate, Kwesi strolled up, bags and tickets in hand. I felt like chewing him out but just turned and boarded the plane without saying much.

We arrived in Greenwich to alarmed World Council of Churches hosts. I was handed a note while someone told me that my court-appointed attorney had made several calls described as "very urgent." I looked down at the paper while listening to an anxious briefing from one of the hosts. The note contained my attorney's name and phone number, with the scribbled words "important; notify upon arrival." I felt that something very disconcerting was afoot. I looked into Kwesi's eyes, which reflected the same *Oh shit, here we go* sense that was swelling up in my chest alongside my rapidly pulsing heartbeat.

We were given access to an office with a phone and some privacy. Kwesi took out a cigarette and lit it while I dialed. In the attorney's official-sounding, matter-of-fact tone were words confirming our instinctive emotions: the US Attorney denied permission to attend the conference, and I had, therefore, violated the terms of my bond and a warrant had been issued for my arrest. My head swam. I had to sit down as he continued.

Kwesi's eyes and mouth were agape. My heart skipped beats as I tried to hold back my breath. The attorney's words rolled on: "They are looking for you and will arrest you. Come back to Dallas, but do not use the airport, train stations, or bus terminals. They're sure to be looking for you in those places." With those last words, I set the phone down, trying to make sense of what was happening. It took a few minutes to repeat the message to Kwesi.

We quickly agreed that we were set up and that the police were using this as a reason to say we were dangerous criminals now, with a more "justifiable" pretext to kill us. It was the summer of 1969, after all. We knew the heat was on; many of our comrades in Dallas and throughout the country were behind bars or being railroaded into long prison stretches. That year more than two dozen Black Panther Party members had been shot and killed. All under provocative and seemingly prefabricated circumstances to justify the use of deadly force.

Kwesi bluntly stated he would not do the time. I nodded and said in as confident a voice as I could pull together: "We'll get through this. We're gonna make it." It took us less than a few minutes to agree to run—not to return to Dallas, but to disappear. We exited the office nook and rejoined our hosts, who were gathering in the conference center. I explained as best I could what we had just learned; that we were reeling from the staggering news and needed to leave immediately for New York. We asked for a ride and were driven to the heart of the city.

It was a hot and muggy afternoon. We found a phone booth on the bustling streets of Manhattan, and called some folk in the Fifth Avenue SNCC offices. We dared not go there. Instead, we were directed to the Village, and to an apartment of a young woman named Carla. She welcomed us and left us alone after providing us with sandwiches and her entire apartment. We dared not use her phone. We made several more calls from a nearby pay phone. The most important call was to my cousin Harry. We were eventually directed to his trusted contact, a brother in Spanish Harlem.

Our hearts were pounding heavily, adrenaline on full blast. We were in fight-or-flight mode, feeling the heat from imminently approaching pursuers, determined to survive whatever came our way. We had only a few dollars, a change of clothes at best, no concrete plans or advanced forethought about what we would or could do next. Still, we had each other, a few trusted comrades, an undeniable cause to wage, and an unspeakable faith. That was sufficient!

The next night, a man named Joe greeted us at his apartment near 88th Street. He was a character with a wry sense of humor who treated Kwesi and me as if we were on a vacation visiting him for a few days. Later that night, we learned that our stay there had to end sooner rather than later. We got an alarming call that a team of armed men "dressed like truck drivers" had kicked in the doors of Carla's Greenwich Village apartment and were looking for us. It was the FBI, armed with warrants for our arrest. If we required any other validations for turning north rather than heading south to Texas, that staggering development sealed the deal: Canada, here we come!

Kwesi and I had no real plans, no clothes, and no money. We were desperate to discover or create a twenty-first century Underground Railroad, one for our own survival.

The Partees (circa 1923): my maternal grandfather, Joe Chavis Partee (lower center), a widower and loving father, surrounded by his children (clockwise from upper center) Arlen Clifton (A.C.), Mildred, Neva, Eva, Annie Faye, and Cecil.

The McMillans (circa 1915): my paternal grandfather Walter Rhee (seated left) with (middle/lower row) son Marion Ernest, wife Meirrell Vain, son Walter C., and daughter Ollie Lee. Top row—sons Walter "Lucky" and Xenophon, and daughter Lillie Mae.

Family in the living room (circa 1950). Me, second from left, with Mom and Dad, sisters Karen, Jackie, and Frosty the dog.

Easter Sunday (circa 1958). Me (far left), with sisters Karen, Jackie, and Kathy along with cousins Harry Wells and Leslie Faye Wells.

Booker T. Washington Technical High School's 1963 Senior class on "Senior Day," celebrating the "Roaring Twenties" (circa May, 1963).

Dallas SNCC (circa 1968): core SNCC activists. Seated are Jackie McMillan Hill, Felicia Johnson, and Eva McMillan. Standing are Eddie Harris, Kaleef Hasan, Bettie Poindexter, Curtis Gaines, Ruth Jefferson, Jackie Harris. Note: Curtis Gaines was later cited as a police informer/agent and excluded from Dallas SNCC.

THE BLACK DISCIPLE

VOL.—1   Dallas, Texas — DEC. 7, 1968   DON. 15 Cents

Black Dallas VS. White "Justice"

With the boycott of the O. K. super markets Black people of South Dallas have made it plain and clear that they will not be the passive and pathetic "Negroes" that Dallas has grown to be known for.

When you stop letting yourself be robbed and exploited by grocery theives , you start looking Black, Beautiful, and bold. When you show that you are fed up with being a chump for White Exploitation, then you have grown aware. When you flex the muscle of unity to end the looting by white businesses you have finally started moving. And so it happened in Dallas. The successful boycott scared White bandits into making a very foolish mistake. They thought that they could crush this new Black movement for strength by making an example of Matthew Johnson and Ernest McMillan who played an active roll in the boycott.

The cold blooded Whites felt that if it could bring their power and vengence to rest on Dallas Sncc, Black Dallas would return to the Tommish habit of meekness. The Community made the Boycott 85% effective, to squash the Community actions. White Power tried and convicted Ernest McMillan and Matthew Johnson and sentenced them to ten years. in prison for breaking a water melon and a gallon of milk. They figured this type retalitation would frighten Black People and run them back into their holes. Black Dallas did they succeed? Today, Dallas SNCC and SNICK attorneys are in the process of appealing the decision of the Dallas County Court, on the basis of many unjust court procedures. Many Black People feel that the Texas Courts are part of a scheme to crush SNCC on a State wide level. For almost at the same time that Ernie & Matt were arrested other (4) Dallas SNCC member were arreasted and are being held on various charges. In Austin, SNCC is metting illegal harrassment that grow out of polotical activity. Austin Community efforts have been stepped up and the University Of Texas studen have joined to support Austin SNCC by organizaning a State raising fund campaign. In Houston the Field Secretary of SNCC was sentenced to 30 yrs in prison, due to a trumped up marijuana possession charge. The rank of Houston SNCC has almost tripled in size since its initiation.

The determined effort on the part of SNCC Activist in Dallas has been just the opposite of what the Power Structure expected.

There can be no doubt that Black people all over the Nation are fed up with deceit and unfairness of White "Justice."

DALLAS SNCC

Excerpts of an edition of *the Black Disciple,* the voice of Dallas SNCC. Editor, Edward "Black Ed" Harris.

FROM THE EDITOR

Dear Brothers and Sisters:

I, along with the staff of the Black Disciple would like to make an apology at this time to our patrons for the temporary discontinuance of our newspaper. Due to pressure on the organization from the downtown power structure we have been unable to operate adequately. Now that we have had time to "Get ourselves together" again, a weekly publication of the Black Disciple will be available to the public from this issue forward.

The Black Disciple is sponsored by the Dallas Student Non-Violent Coordinating Committee which is a non-profit making organization. All funds appropriated through this newspaper will be used to support the paper, and aid in financing Dallas SNCC's community programs and activities. The purpose of this newspaper is to relate to the Black community, as accurate as possible, information on international, national, State, city, and community affairs that are relevant to Black people.

We welcome all subscribers to write and inform us of your likes and dislikes concerning the publication of your newspaper.

Freedom and Peace,
Editor--Ed Harris

"TO BE"

Into the deepest pits of darkness,

"Black is", where light has
        never shown before.

That which is the secret of
        strength,

Perpetuated by knowledge to be
        found there in.

To light the torch for the search
        is to provide Life's
        nourishment for the
        living dead.

But the true feast my NIGGER
        son shall not come
        till every torch is
        aflame.

THE BLACK DISCIPLE

The Black Disciple is published once weekly. Subscription rates are $10.00 per year or $5.00 per 6 months (patron subscription) and $7.25 per year or $3.75 per 6 months (regular subscription). Address all correspondence to P.O. Box 22063, Dallas, Texas 75202.

Ed Harris, Publisher-Editor
Linda Coleman, Secretary

Excerpts of an edition of *the Black Disciple,* the voice of Dallas SNCC. Editor, Edward "Black Ed" Harris.

DISCIPLE • PAGE SEVEN

Letter From The "NAM"

Dear Mom & Family,

I am supposed to tell you that I am well and doing fine with no immediate worries or dangers. That our role here is a good and constructive one, that these poor starving people are overjoyed at our being here. But Mom, I can't do it. I have to let someone in "the world" know what's going on . It might cost me a court-martial, but being in the brig(jail) is 100 times better than watching these pigs torture, rape, murder, mame, and exploit a people who are as oppressed as my own people are. Mom, I can't describe the revulsion I felt yesterday when our company commander ordered the napalming of an entire village, roasting alive everything there because he thought he'd seen a suspected viet cong run into it. Nor can I tell you how I felt at seeing a viet cong, after being blown to pieces by a grenade, have his ears cut off for some honkie to take home as souvenirs.

I made a mistake by coming here, but, at this time, I believed that bullshit they were feeding me about "allegiance to my country". A country that I have far more dangerous enemies in than I do here. A country that practice total genocide for a people that built it. No Mom, I can't write you the lies I am suppose to write. about the hot meals, cleans clothes, and hot bathes, for you see, these things are pleasures I read dream about. Have you ever smelled a man that has not bathed in 3 weeks? Ever seen a man jump at the chance to eat anything?

A dog, cat, monkey meat, water buffalo, raw fish, or an occasional fat rat. C-rations are okay I guess you get used to them if you eat them often enough but it seems that they aren't any to plentiful.

Well Mom, I'm going to have to close for now. It's starting to rain again and I have no place to go to get out of it and this paper isn't waterproof. Tell little brother whatever he's doing to keep doing it and let this man's army alone. It seems that Uncle Sam just doesn' take good care of his "children". Love to Pop and all our friends.

Your Son,
The Grunt

P.S.

Hey Mom, could you send me some sardines or peanut butter or something to eat? The monkies have started to get wise.

BLACK THOUGHT...

Living means love.
Living includes work and conflict.
How can you love if you do not face and resist the forces of destruction?
Such a course requires courage, and courage is a true value.

DISCIPLE • PAGE THREE

SNCC Make Plans For
CULTURAL CENTER

The Dallas Chapter of SNCC has begun making plans for a Black Cultural Center to be established in one of the several Black communities in Dallas. Its" purpose will be to install self awareness into the minds of our young black brothers and sisters who will undoubtedly be the salvation of the Black Man's true pride and dignity. The school will also be available to the older segment of the community as they might see the need to learn more of their past history and heritage. The liberation school will be designed to inform the Black man, who blames all his problems on the white man, that the fault lies in himself. The Black Man has not come to manhood because he does not know himself. By not teaching the Black man of himself, the present educational system has failed to deal realistically with the needs of the ghetto.

The "drop out" rate among young people in the black community is growing. SNCC attributes this lack of interest in getting an education to the failure of those institutions to formulate a curriculum that would begin to fill the emptiness that exist in every Black Man's soul, and to shake the enslavement that walls in every Black Man's mind.

The Cultural Center should be a great asset to the growth and stability of the Black community. Dallas SNCC therefore anticipates tremendous support for the school.

McMillan Released
On Bond

November 16, 1968. Marion Ernest McMillan was released from the Dallas County Jail on a $5,000 personal appearance bond, after being indicted for an alleged draft evasion. McMillan's bond was secured by American Civil Liberties Union with the support of a biracial group of interested Dallas citizens. A previous bond of $10,000 was posted Nov. 8, 1968 for charges of accumting to $143,00 for which McMillan and Matthew Johnson were convicted and sentenced to 10 years imprisonment, due to their political involvement as black community organizers.

The bond for the draft evasion charge was originally set at $10,000. A bond hearing was held November 13, which resulted in a reduction of the bond to $5,000. One of the Attorney's for the defense stated to a _Disciple Reporter_ there was a rumor going around that McMillan would not be out of jail too long.

The charges of both McMillan and Johnson are now being appealed.

THE REAL PROBLEM
"They're so busy killing niggers they cant even see us!!;"

Excerpts of an edition of *the Black Disciple,* the voice of Dallas SNCC. Editor, Edward "Black Ed" Harris.

'Victory' Claimed

Welfare Sit-in Ends in 3 Days

By MARYLN SCHWARTZ and JOHN GEDDIE

Negro welfare protesters ended a 3-day sit-in at the state welfare offices Wednesday night, claiming "victory" and vowing to reorganize for further "action and victories" in their fight for increased welfare payments and better treatment.

"We are not giving up," said Mrs. Ruth Jefferson, spokesman for the group of protesting mothers. "We have won this victory. We are now going to go out and get more support and reorganize."

Earlier in the afternoon, Mrs. Jefferson talked directly with the office of Health, Education and Welfare in Washington which, after hearing her list of 12 grievances,

Related Story on Page 17A.

promised to send in a 4- or 5-member team from HEW to investigate the situation. The team will arrive Friday morning.

Mrs. Jefferson announced the group's intention to leave at 8:45 p.m., claiming "victory" in the federal government's agreement to investigate her complaints.

AMONG the group's demands were those for $100 welfare a month per child, more black welfare workers, an allowance for winter clothing and the opportunity to be treated with "dignity and democracy."

During the afternoon the protesters were served with legal papers ordering them to appear in court Dec. 5 to show cause why they should not be held in contempt of court for remaining in the state welfare offices after receiving orders to leave.

Dist. Judge Hoyet Armstrong approved the latest order for the show-cause hearing, filed by the state attorney general's office. It named 29 persons, but "John Doe" papers were prepared for unidentified protesters.

Mrs. Jefferson announced that the protesters would be having a Thanksgiving dinner Thursday at the Mt. Olive Lutheran Church, 3100 Forest. She urged persons offering support to get in touch with the group at the church. The group was supported during its sit-in by members of the Student Non-Violent Coordinating Committee.

THE STATE welfare offices, meanwhile, were in the process of being moved Wednesday night from 3306 Main Street—site of the sit-in—to new offices at the Old Red Courthouse building on Record.

Movers cleared out all furniture except the tables and chairs in the room occupied by the protesters.

In connection with the move, county commissioners Wednesday night gave Sheriff Bill Decker full authority to do "whatever is necessary" to keep the demonstrators out of the old courthouse.

At a specially called meeting in the Dallas County Courthouse, commissioners ordered Decker to "deny entry to any county building by unauthorized personnel after business hours."

Commissioner Frank Crowley said he felt no group, no matter what their intentions, should be allowed in a government building after closing time.

County Judge Lew Sterrett agreed, saying: "I have been most anxious to give our sheriff the power to protect the property of the public during this period."

THE SIT-IN drew Dr. George Wiley, executive director of the National Welfare Rights Organization with headquarters in Washington, D.C., here Wednesday morning. He said he had been asked by the local group to come and help the mothers with their protest.

Also arriving was Carl Rachlin of New York, a noted civil rights attorney and the general counsel for the welfare rights organization.

Wiley told a press conference that his group plans to show that the state-imposed maximum of $80 million for welfare funds was not legal. He said the next step would be to have a special session of the state Legislature called so that more money could be appropriated for welfare.

"The welfare problem in Texas is greater than in most states because the state has been oppressive for so long," he said. "We figure there is about $30 million in funds that could be appropriated to welfare right now but isn't. There are only about 25 per cent of the people in the state that should be on welfare that actually are on welfare."

The Dallas campaign, he said, is part of the NWRO's "Winter Action Campaign" in 25 cities across the country.

"The campaign is spotlighting the recipients' nationwide action for money for poor people—now," said Wiley.

Article in the *Dallas Morning News* on the SNCC-led three-day occupation of the Dallas welfare offices.

With cohort Kwesi Williams; exiled "fugitives" in West Africa (circa 1969).

Escorted to the Dallas County Jail in cuffs by Dallas Deputy Sheriff after capture in Cincinnati, Ohio, December 1971.

A cherished visit with Felicia and baby Ernest Ohene Kitiwa while imprisoned at Federal Correctional Institute, Texarkana Texas (circa 1972).

Testifying to the Texas Legislature in Austin, Texas (circa 1975) along with members of CURE (Citizens United for the Rehabilitation of Errants).

PHOTO BY ALAN POGUE – WWW.DOCUMENTARYPHOTOGRAPHS.COM

PART THREE:

ON THE RUN

Canada, Africa,
and Returning Home

CHAPTER NINE

MY WORLD WAS SCALDED BY the murders of the four Birmingham girls, by the killing of Malcolm X, Dr. King, the three civil rights workers slain in Mississippi, and by the unpublicized murder of George Bess, a dear friend and comrade killed there a month later. Following the call for Black Power, there were even more intensive attacks, as J. Edgar Hoover's strategy for counterinsurgency unfolded. In 1969 alone, there were more than two dozen police executions of Black Panthers, armed attacks on members of the Republic of New Afrika, scores of movement leaders imprisoned, and others forced into exile. Kwesi and I now found ourselves among THE EXILED.

We made it to Montreal and found support within a small cluster of Canadian peace activists, who provided a set of temporary lodgings throughout several neighborhoods, with the most notable and lasting stay in a Greek neighborhood I recall being on the northside of Montreal. Although it was July, the climate and the streets felt cold to us. Our only defense, if confronted by any law enforcement, was the pair of driver's licenses obtained along the way belonging to two very real persons—one from Massachusetts and the other from New York. Their driver's licenses identified us as law-abiding US citizens.

Once in Montreal, we ran into another problem. We felt we needed hardware—guns, ammunition—to respond to the highly likely attempts to arrest, imprison, or assassinate us. We needed guns, but our underground hosts either tried to convince us we did not need them or had no real links to them. In our search, we met a young Black Canadian man in a bar. After feeling him out, we asked him where we could get ahold of some pieces. He simply asked what kind, how many, and how much we wanted to pay for them. He promised he could get us two .45 automatics for a couple of hundred dollars. We jumped in a cab with him, he gave the cab driver an intersection as our destination. Upon arrival at this urban tenement, the driver pulled over, and our guy "Rocky" asked for the money. We balked. Kwesi and I looked at each other incredulously and then at Rocky who said, "Look, these people will not go through with any of this, let alone open their doors to me with you there, or anywhere in sight." Though we were newbies to Canada, to the streets of Montreal, there is an indisputable law of universal proportions that says do not buy a pig in a poke.

But we succumbed to desperation and fears of being naked in the streets, and despite only knowing this guy for less than an hour, we forked over the money to him. He told the cabbie and us to wait fifteen minutes, got out of the cab, and disappeared around the corner. Disappeared! We got out of the cab, sent the taxi on its way, and began a fruitless search for Rocky. We turned the corner, walked up and down the streets, through alleys and gave up. Suckers we were.

We turned our attention to finding a phone booth and calling a cab. We found it, and as I dug in my pocket to find a coin and dial, the Montreal PD pulled up, lights flashing, demanding our ID and our business there at this early morning hour. We handed them our newly acquired driver's licenses, while one reported that there was a very recent bomb explosion at a postal station nearby. So now we were suspected terrorists, placed in the patrol car and driven to a police station. After a series of questions by the Royal Canadian Mounted Police, the Mounties, they left us and huddled into a corner. They had asked for the names and phone numbers of people who could vouch for us, our activities in Montreal. They also wanted to know where we were staying, to which we responded that we were going to find a hotel when we were detained. Their next question:

where was our luggage? As fate, or pure luck, would have it, our luggage was in storage at the bus station. I had three tickets for our three pieces of baggage. Somehow, I managed to hand the Mounties two of the three tickets for the bags that only held our clothes), while palming one—the one that held the most incriminating evidence: Texas newspaper clippings about our fugitive state that we'd use for future hosts—support referrals; movement literature; and a black book of old and new national and international contacts. By the grace of God, the police ended up searching at the bus station and found only the most innocent-looking bags.

We also provided them with the names and phone numbers of two Canadian women, McGill University students we met a day or two before. The two college students were more than beneficial to our plight as they not only informed the police that they indeed knew us as reputable persons, but were outraged that the police would jail us. They said they believed we were victims of racial profiling. The Mounties returned our IDs and our luggage and handed us an official document we were required to present at the Canadian border within forty-eight hours. If we failed to depart Canada, presenting that document as proof of our departure, arrest warrants would be issued, and we would be regarded as criminals or at least illegal immigrants.

We left the station in total, momentary relief, ripped up the document, and vowed to find new Canadian identification as soon as possible. We had no plans to leave Canada just yet.

The way we got to Nova Scotia, with the FBI on our trail, was a miracle. In one instance, a group of organized taxi drivers took us from Montreal, relaying us by cab, from point to other point, onto the next, all the way to Quebec City. My cousin Harry, who was in college writing a thesis on economics at the University of Guelph, became our number one go-to.

Harry was three months younger than I was and grew up in the Elm Thicket neighborhood in Dallas. He was always bigger than me, a great conversationalist, and a superb athlete, playing football and basketball.

His athleticism became his tool to further his education because, at heart, he was an intellectual.

We spent a lot of time together growing up before he moved to Los Angeles in ninth grade. We were more like brothers, attending movies together, roller skating, dating girls. I have fond memories of his mom, my Aunt Fay, cooking lavish breakfasts for us when I would sleep over. It was at his home that I was introduced to the Black street culture because his family listened to more popular Black radio stations and were more in tune with all the happenings. At my house, we listened to the news.

Harry received a scholarship to USC to study and play football, where he was an All-American and blocker for O. J. Simpson, until his exciting football career ended after breaking his foot twice. After college, he married and moved to Canada to work on his master's degree and then a PhD. In 1969, he took a sabbatical from school to help me stay alive. He appointed himself the hand for Kwesi and me surviving and navigating our way through exile—to Africa and back. Harry would be our lifeline, our connection to the world.

He shared with us that the sacrifice was worth it, as he admired me for what I was doing. He knew the fight for justice and civil rights was important. I knew, however, that Harry would have been Dr. Harry Wells if it were not for me.

In Canada, my brave cousin Harry helped us secure Canadian passports, using names from cemeteries of Blacks who had died in Nova Scotia to secure birth certificates. He also got a Catholic priest to sign the documents. We met students in Montreal, who then introduced us to revolutionaries, members of the Front de libération du Québec (FLQ). They were determined to make Quebec a free, self-determining French state. While there, Kwesi and I had a narrow escape at a bus station in Montreal after a bombing. We were arrested and interrogated by the police, who wanted to search our bags. By the grace of God, the police ended up searching through the bags that held only our clothes and not our real documentation. Finally, we had successfully changed our identities. We were now ready to make our way to France, bound for West Africa, in hopes of gaining political asylum in Guinea.

•

It was my first time on African soil. I landed on the runway at the Bamako airport in Mali, alone. In Paris, Kwesi and I had decided to separate, mainly due to inadequate finances. I could now only hope he was safe on the Canary Islands with a sister, a Black teacher from California, he met and magically clicked with while we were briefly in Paris. We agreed that I would proceed ahead, to make headway in breaking the logjam we encountered with the embassy in France, a situation fraught with hindrances obstructing us from entering the liberated zone of the Republic of Guinea.

The plane had a bumpy landing, but I felt exhilarated, finally on the ground in Africa. I deplaned the Air France jet under a scorching sun and joined the other passengers walking along the tarmac toward the terminal. I felt compelled to stop, kneel and press my lips onto the earth that radiated steaming waves of heat into the arid atmosphere. I felt I belonged there. I was a prodigal son who had found his way home. Even though I was on my knees in Mother Africa, I was a man with a compass pointing east. From those very first days in Canada and ever since, our main intent was to enter Guinea.

The Guinean Embassy in Mali, its bordering neighbor, was where I aimed to receive a visa to join forces with Stokely Carmichael, blazing a trail for Kwesi to enter the country, too. Mali was not the ultimate destination, only step three of what I prayed would be the last leg for securing refuge in revolutionary Guinea. Its leader, President Ahmed Sekou Touré, possessed a heroic stature and his voice resounded loud and clear to all who fought for African Liberation. He was a leader who stood tall against colonial powers and their superpower backer, the United States of America. Stokely honored the man and his legacy not only in obtaining dual citizenship but also by transforming himself into "a son of Africa." In fact, he was no longer Stokely Carmichael, but Kwame Touré. His activism and road to Africa was impressive, from SNCC to "Honorary Prime Minister" of the Black Panther Party and leader of the All-African People's Revolutionary Party. Here I was, following his lead.

I cleared customs as a Canadian citizen, stepped into a scrum of hawkers and vendors, and began looking for a taxi. There was a line of cabbies and in my high-school, southern-dialect French, I managed to ask one to take me to a good, cheap hotel. Without further questioning, the driver took me to the Grand Hotel. A "grand" hotel it was: a large, luxurious palace, with porters, marble floors, and sweeping verandas to greet me. I nervously approached the receptionist, a gracious middle-aged African gentleman. He asked for my passport, the number of people in my party, and the number of days I intended to stay. While handing him my passport, I told him I would be there about a week, possibly longer. I signed a form and that was it. No request for credit card, cash, or deposit.

Once in my room, I immediately checked my pockets, which contained a few French francs, and fell asleep on a king-size bed under a gently whirling ceiling fan. I awoke later that evening in a darkened room, feeling starved. I walked to the dining room where a waiter greeted me. There were just a few people in the large dining area, a space that could easily accommodate ten times the number. There was an abundance of servers, too, with at least three people attending to me, bringing water, menus, wine lists. I declined the wine, decided to order only soup and bread, and prayed I had enough to cover the meager meal. The bill arrived and as I dug in my pocket for my francs, the waiter smiled and asked me to just sign and indicate my room number. I left him a very nice tip, considering his and my own economic conditions. Throughout my stay, the waiters would pocket my tips. Later, the hotel learned they had treated me with free meals during my entire stay. In fact, it was the first and last time I would eat such a light meal there.

The next morning, I awoke excited to visit the Guinean Embassy. The morning sun was beaming, and I eagerly started on my trek to Embassy Row. I arrived early and discovered they had not yet opened their doors, so I explored a bit more and found a place to wait at an open-air cafe. The only seats were a set of wobbly stools at a wooden bar. A few folks were standing, drinking tea or coffee, and I asked for a cup and placed a few coins on the counter. There were flies whizzing by and crawling along my ears and arms. I was the only one who even attempted to swat at them, shoo them away. It was a hopeless battle, but one I intended to wage. Suddenly, one fly dove into my cup of tea. I was pissed. I beckoned to the attendant, pointing to the fly now back-stroking in my cup of hot tea. He looked at my cup of tea, back at me, and then back at the tea. He picked up a spoon, nonchalantly flicked the fly out, then turned and walked away. I surrendered and left, unable to take another sip.

Later, I joined the line outside the embassy and stood waiting with my Canadian passport and a manila envelope containing copies of my real ID and news clippings from America's reporting on my absconding in hand. Eventually, I was seated with a junior clerk, who was in no mood for long explanations or stories, especially from someone with a Canadian passport, claiming *not* to be the person on the passport, but instead with some sob story about seeking political asylum. The clerk looked at me for a moment and said, "Come back tomorrow," which would soon become a familiar refrain for me. I was dumbfounded. Over the next several days, I began to feel as if air and hope were being sucked out of me. I was slowly being drained of the energy it would take for me to move forward, to survive. I did not know what to do next.

It did not help that I also felt isolated from Malian society. The people spoke an entirely different language than the French I barely spoke, and worshipped Islam, a religion I knew nothing about. The lifestyles were too formal, way too rigid for me to introduce myself to strangers. I walked the streets in the hot sun, feeling lost and alone. One day, I found a park, spotted a raggedy bench, and sat down in the limited shade. As I took in the scene, I noticed the shadows of large birds circling above me. I looked up to discover a flock of vultures gliding together in a slow, choreographed dance of nature's flight. They seemed to be drawn to something nearby. My eyes roamed a full 360 degrees in search of hints of a dead carcass. Suddenly and gracefully, with a bit of deliberate caution, one after another the vultures descended, touching down about fifty feet from me. As they slowly moved their huge claws in my direction, I finally realized I was the object of their desires. Panicked, I got up from the bench and hastily returned to the hotel, never looking back.

Back at the Grand Hotel, I saw a gray-haired, distinguished-looking white man sitting in the dining room. He stood and greeted me as I neared, inviting me to join him for dinner. He shared that he had been in Mali for a few days and had seen me in the dining room eating alone. I acquiesced and joined him for a good meal and conversation. Turns out, he was Irish and felt a sense of commonality with Black Americans. It hit home. It dawned on me that Canada is a North American nation and I, being an African from North America, was just as African American as any Black person of Brazil, Cuba, Mexico, or Peru, not simply the United States. Over the next few days, he confided in me more and I in him. We would sit for long stretches at the bar, at meals and outside the hotel. I learned he fervently supported the IRA (the Irish Republican Army) which, during those times, was waging urban guerilla warfare in Ireland and throughout Great Britain. He never detailed his relationship with the IRA, nor his "business" dealings in Mali. I never explained my legal standings or affiliations either. We seemed to share a strong bond of solidarity for each other and our respective struggles against colonialism and the rule of empires. We both were fighting for the right and the power of self-determination. In Africa, I had found an unlikely ally, in a white man.

•

When he joined me a week or so later in Mali, Kwesi and I found ourselves on the run again. Together once more, 6,065 miles from our homes in Dallas. We were traveling by road in a lorry bound for Ghana, following the generous lead and miraculous invitation from a few young Ghanaians we met back in Bamako. They were bound for Germany in search of work, while Kwesi and I were traveling in the opposite direction, toward Accra, Ghana, to the city they left behind.

Donned in dashikis, we carried small pieces of hand luggage, feeling comfortable and confident that we could easily blend in among the other travelers and pilgrims on the African road. We were wrong. The lorry driver and his assistants automatically treated us as foreigners, as we were given the first-class seats inside the truck, alongside the driver rather than in the truck panel that was congested with passengers sitting on wooden planks that served as seats. The other passengers were crammed with their luggage, along with live chickens and dead monkeys. Without ever opening our mouths, it seemed Kwesi and I were viewed as strangers, outsiders, even as *Oburoni*, or "white men."

The road was bumpy and we traveled only during daylight hours, camping out near the road in towns or villages at night. We would find an open park or a market square where people did not seem to mind our presence. Sometimes, small groups of men would sit and converse with us. A few would either speak a little English, navigate my poor French, use non-verbal expressions, or employ an impressive combination of them all. At one overnight stopover in an Upper Volta village, the conversation "got good" with the aid of a little herb. We exchanged stories about America and what was really happening back home. Kwesi and I tried our best to debunk the lies and propaganda about America many Africans so very passionately chose to cling to, such as the abundance of big cars, nice homes, easy money, and the glamorous living that they assumed *everyone* enjoyed. They did not want to hear about oppression, injustices, lynchings, enslavement, police brutality, and the ever-widening income gap.

Many were courteous and patient as they listened to example after example of racism, poverty, and inequality in America. Sometimes, they would wince or recoil, evidently feeling the sting and the pain of what we had recounted. But after all was said and done, once we had exhausted ourselves sharing the facts, figures, personal accountings, and story after story about the crimes against humanity faced daily by the masses in the United States, our African brothers and sisters never failed to ask, "So how can I go and live there?" It was so frustrating, almost maddening for Kwesi and me to realize the addictive depths and never dwindling hope and burning desire many held to go to America, a place we fled!

At one of our very first full rest stops, we pulled over near what appeared to be a marketplace to stretch our legs and grab a bite to eat. I was more thirsty than hungry and was delighted to see a stand with Coke bottles filled with a clear liquid, topped with a lemon stuffed into the bottle. I thought this was a perfect cure for the blazing sun, some nice citrusy juice for the worn and weary traveler. While Kwesi searched for food, I gravitated to this refreshing stand. I pulled a few Malian coins from my robe's pockets and held out my hand for the vendors to pick the number of coins needed to pay for two bottles of the mysterious drink. The woman attending looked puzzled, so I grabbed two bottles and held them next to my open palm with the coins. She looked around confused and after some sort of affirmation by her co-vendors, she shrugged her shoulders and picked a few coins from my hand.

I turned to walk away with my new purchase. I did not see Kwesi right away, so I walked back across the street and sat alongside the lorry to have a sip. I put one bottle down beside me and took the other, pulling the lemon from the bottle and prepared to take a swig. It seemed as if the entire marketplace grew silent. Everyone stopped moving and turned his or her attention in my direction. I looked around and smiled. Perhaps, I thought, they have never had such a customer as me, a foreigner who appreciated their quaint culture and could enjoy their products. It took only one sip of the warm, thick substance to realize I was not drinking a refreshing fruit juice, but thick, greasy, sticky cooking oil! I provided my audience with the performance of the month, perhaps of the year, as they roared with delight and amusement as I spat out the oil, rubbing my mouth vigorously and looked around helplessly, ashamed. Kwesi returned and quickly surmised the situation, joining in the chorus of laughter. He added insult to injury, by pointing his finger at me and holding up the bottle for all to better see, asking, "Man, what were you thinking?"

We continued our bumpy drive toward Ghana. We were seldom on any paved road and virtually never on any road that could be deemed a highway. We traveled through the bush, in and out of lush forests, and over rolling hills. Suddenly, we came to a screeching halt a few hours away from Ghana's border. An eighteen-wheeler lay sprawled on its side blocking any path around it. Everyone got off our lorry and walked toward the disabled vehicle. There was no sense of how long the truck had been in this predicament, as there was no fire, smoke, or smell of gas fumes. No one appeared injured, though the driver paced around the truck, pondering the damages and scratching his head. There was no apparent cargo, just an empty trailer. People began to gather in highly animated discussion, in words we could not comprehend. There were, however, clear undeniable gestures indicating a collective recourse was being hotly debated. Folks began to emerge from all directions and gathered at the truck. A few began to pull at nearby tree limbs while others began hacking away at large branches. Someone approached with rope and our driver pulled out links of chain from some undetected secret compartment under the lorry. Suddenly, it became apparent to Kwesi and me that no one was thinking of waiting for first responders—*we* were the first and only responders.

Soon, a soft chant was swelling from the gatherers. Someone threw lengths of rope over the truck while others began fastening them to the vehicle. Others began to push rods, limbs, and even whole tree trunks beside and under the truck to use as levers. People continued to show up from cars and trucks ahead and behind us. Kwesi and I joined the swirling vortex, grabbing a section of the crippled semi. With backs leaning, ropes and chains tautly pulling, and the new levers digging in, a rocking motion began. In a mounting synchronicity, a unison of voices, muscles, hands, and backs began to dislodge the side of the truck from the earth. Slowly but steadily, the ground began to release its metal prisoner and up, up, up it rose from ground level toward the sky. Chants rose more determinedly, like a possessed choir and then—*wham*—the truck was upright again! Cheers and a roaring laughter rose from all around, as everyone exchanged hugs and embraces. Then, without a visible signal, or any motion to adjourn that I could discern, the community of helpers faded back into the bush and back into their vehicles and the once-disabled truck and its driver began chugging toward their destination once more.

Kwesi and I stood looking around and then at each other, mouths agape, our heads shaking in disbelief, sweat mixed with salty tears pouring down our faces. We were astounded by the act of unity and community we had just experienced. After a moment, we returned to our first-class seats on the jam-packed lorry and began rumbling once again from somewhere in this, the ever so fertile Niger River .Valley, bound for our next destination.

Revolutionary Algeria was an option for us. It had recently succeeded in defeating French colonial rule. They expressed support for the Black Liberation movement. The country granted several Black Panthers political asylum and hosted the Pan African summit. Reaching Algeria from Mali by land, however, meant traversing the Sahara. The image of the two of us dragging over thousands of miles of sand dunes under the unblinking, scorching rays of the sun, without a guide or a road, let alone a road map, caused us to ditch that idea.

We settled on Ghana. It was a no-brainer going to Ghana from Mali, as we had a contact there, Ghanaians spoke English, and we would still have options of going to Guinea or Tanzania. At the time, Julius Nyerere, a highly progressive, independent-thinking father of African Unity and communal socialist society, led Tanzania.

•

The lorry we mounted in Bamako safely brought Kwesi and me to the Ghanaian border with Upper Volta. Upon our arrival, we presented our phony IDs and had our baggage searched. We were questioned about our literature, particularly our books about Pan-Africanism, the African revolution, Kwame Nkrumah, and Frantz Fanon, all of which they viewed as suspicious and even dangerous. The uniformed border agent threatened to take them from us, so we gave him a few dollars in order to keep them and enter the country without incident. Frustrated and tired, Kwesi began to argue with the man about our rights and freedom. I tugged at his arm and led him away as the agent (not so covertly) pocketed our scarce funds.

It was easy to locate the Sawyer family once we arrived in Accra. Our only real clues were that they lived near the central post office. We were treated so kindly, as everyone we approached was ever so gracious and welcoming. We were happy and relieved to finally speak English and delighted in the Ghanaian's openness to our requests for help. The words of the young men we met days earlier who were en route to Germany and spoke of Ghanaians "loving strangers" was proving true as Kwesi and I were escorted to the doorsteps of the Sawyers' family home.

The Sawyers resided in an enclosed compound on a busy street. Turns out that the paternal head of the household, Mr. Sawyer, had at least two wives and several children of varying ages, from toddlers to young adults, by each. He was a retired businessman and the family lived seemingly well on his savings and the income generated by the wives in the marketplace. There was a small garden, chickens, and even a few goats within the compound. Each wife had her own apartment with their children. The adults welcomed Kwesi and I, while the children bounded around us, looking on with big smiles. We were given a small room of our own, shown where to use the bathroom and shower, and were served a fine meal of fried fish and rice.

We spent three or more months in Accra with the Sawyer family. Whenever we would retrieve a few dollars from home (through mail routed surreptitiously through several states and countries to reach us finally under an anonymous name with real addresses), we would share a portion with the family. We had no steady income, no jobs, but from time to time I would join the fishermen along the coastline, located just walking distance from the compound. There, I would lend a hand in hauling in the fishing nets and stand by for anything they would apportion to me. They were always gracious in their giving. Shrimp was not on their list of favorite foods, so I typically wound up with them as leftovers, once they had taken the needlefish, cowfish, rays, eels, and turtles from the net. I would happily bag up my goodies and bring them to my temporary home to share with the household and add to our meals.

While in Ghana, there were many stories told to us about the days of Nkrumah. He was beloved, but even more than that. Many saw him as an immortal man with vast powers. Some even believed he had powerful magic. Nkrumah managed to bring about liberation from British rule with little violence or bloodshed, compared to the many other African anti-colonial struggles. He relied on the threat of violence, the press, organized labor, and unified tribal support, while utilizing boycotts, demonstrations, and high-level negotiations to wrestle Ghana free from the British.

I was told that he would sometimes bring youth and children to the presidential palace once the country was independent and under his leadership. He would allow them to tour the palace grounds and greet them in his spacious meeting room. Once there, Nkrumah would ask them if they were hungry, and the children would enthusiastically affirm such. He would then ask them to bow their heads and pray for food, which they did. The children would remain silent and prayerful for some time then look around to see if there was any food. When it was obvious no food had materialized, Nkrumah asked them to ask him for food. He would beam a broad smile and raise his arms after the children gleefully requested the president give them food. He clapped his hands and a parade of food servers would enter the chamber to fill it with all sorts of scrumptious dishes to the children's delight.

Nkrumah affectionately became known as "Osagyefo," a Fanti word for "redeemer," or highest redeemer. In 1968, he was overthrown by an armed coup financed by the United States (via the CIA) and the chocolate industry. Both bankrolled Ghanaian generals and the police commissioner to stage the coup, allegedly for millions of dollars. I was astonished by how this could take place and asked how the people responded to the coup. I was told most were fearful. On the fateful day, many hid under their beds while gunfire raged outside. The only resistance came from the presidential guard of about three hundred men, who fought valiantly but were heavily outnumbered and completely overwhelmed.

From all accounts, this resounded within me as a loud echo and a realization that the true costs of waging a struggle for liberation is in building living interpenetrating relationships, free of egotistical leadership or an elite. For, without dynamic connection with the people themselves, or being immersed together, wholeheartedly engaged with a collective, grassroots leadership, and an internally shared vision and understanding, any gains are short-lived and soon lost. The struggle must continue to build a circle of trust and whirlpools of participatory connections, without a hierarchy of control, codified beliefs, or a charismatic leader.

CHAPTER TEN

Kwesi and I were tiny dots amid more than one million other dots. We were non-Ghanaians on a road to nowhere; rejects of Kofi Busia, the newly elected President of Ghana, who in a classic blunder and an obstinate attempt to "promote economic growth," decided to expel all aliens from the country, so that hundreds of thousands of idle and unemployed native Ghanaians would possess leftover businesses and jobs. The impact of this newly enacted policy was catastrophic. The very fabric of Ghanaian economy relied on the very natural divisions of labor and the interactivities of all the various tribes and nationalities.

The vitality of the Ghanaian marketplace was the synergy emanating out of African diversity, a kind of unity without uniformity. Each tribe had a specialty of sorts. Some raised cattle. Another herded sheep and goat. There were fishing tribes and other complementary farming cultures. Other tribes were known by their signature crafts: there were jewelers, wood sculptors, fabric and clothing designers. Still others were merchants and traders. Yet with the implementation of Busia's Alien Removal Act, hundreds of thousands—without regard to their individual or peculiar circumstances—were forced to pack and leave at once.

Kwesi and I—being fugitive US citizens documented illegally as Canadians, without connections to any powerful legal or political Ghanaian advocate, and without the cash to bribe the authorities or gatekeepers to circumvent our plight—had to hit the road, too. We decided to head for Liberia, a small country founded by freed slaves from America, rich in natural resources like iron ore, palm oil, bauxite, and rubber. It was ruled and pimped by the notorious dictator William Tubman, a direct descendant of former American-held slaves.

Liberia was also rich in diamonds. Despite its vast natural wealth, Liberia was the third-lowest economy in the world. It was also the African headquarters for Firestone and U.S. Steel, two giant corporations who carried out a systematic rape of the country's most valued natural resources, rubber, and iron ore, twenty-four seven, 365 days every year. Moreover, there existed legalized corruption, as every area of government seemed to be for sale. Anyone with money could purchase registration for a Liberian flag and thereby be able to sail international waters legally as a registered vessel of the country without any checks or safeguards in the way of safety, cargo regulation, public scrutiny. Therefore, Liberia, although one of the planet's poorest nations, technically owned the world's largest shipping fleet.

Although we detested the government of Liberia, the plight of its people, and its puppet role for the Western world, under our present circumstances it made sense—sound geographical and common survival sense—to go there. Only the Ivory Coast stood between it and Ghana, and English was the official language of Liberia. Most importantly, it shared a border with Guinea, our ultimate African destination. Our very new African experience was teaching us how language was a barrier. Mali was the perfect example. The representatives of the Guinean Embassy whom we tried so hard to meet and convince of our circumstances and genuine motives, communicated in French only. Language differences isolated us from the people. *Our* people.

Our plan was to leave Ghana and travel northwest by road though the Ivory Coast to Liberia and its capital city of Monrovia, where we would engage the Guinean Embassy for an entry visa there. Though this was our best prospect for success, the plan seemed far-fetched as we were now stalled among a mass of "foreign rejects" at the Ivory Coast border. Everything had come to a screeching halt. The Ivory Coast forbade anyone from entering and the Ghanaian government refused to let anyone turn back. We were stuck somewhere on that invisible line called "the border," an imaginary line that edged between two nations. Kwesi and I sat on the ground next to our lorry truck, waiting on greater powers to decide our fate. At some point, I heard one lorry cranking up in the distance, then another, then a swarm of engines churning. Then the caravan of trucks, bikes, pedestrians, and ox-drawn carts that had been motionless throughout the night began to move. Without any fanfare or announcement, the border gates opened, and we all began to cross over into Ivory Coast, heading to its capital city, Abidjan.

We were now down to very little cash, having taken a big hit in our already short supply, after converting our Ghanaian money, the new cedi, into the francs of the *Cote d'Ivoire* through the scalpers at the border. We barely grasped the value of Ghana's cedi, let alone managed to fathom the worth of the Ivory Coast franc and, thus, sold our strange cedi for an even more unknown franc. Did we have pearls or poop? We only knew that we had to have francs to eat; our new hosts turned their noses up at the cedi, welcoming it about as much as one would appreciate new rainfall during a flood. As refugees, we were always subject to the mercies and moods of our new hosts. It seemed, however, wherever we went angels mysteriously appeared to protect, nourish, and sustain us.

We entered Abidjan as the sun began its descent into the warm ocean waters. The streets of Abidjan were bustling with a strange new choreography of traffic, pedestrians loaded with heavy objects balanced beautifully on their heads, trucks spewing dark vapors, taxis zipping, and carts zig-zagging in and out of V- and Y-shaped intersections, circular streets, and bustling thoroughfares. As the sunlight faded, a sense of urgency rose within us. Kwesi and I could wind up sleeping on the poorly lit streets. There were no neon signs declaring cafe, hotel, food, or danger, thus offering us few clues for what may lie inside the buildings. We finally entered one and got lucky by using gut instinct and our noses. We happened upon a restaurant! We sat down amid the rumblings of conversations, laughter, and music.

A middle-aged man, made curious by our alien looks, puzzled by our even more foreign sounding tongues or demeanor, or sympathetically motivated by our "I am desperately lost" facial expressions, came over to our little wooden table and said something in French to us. Turns out, he was an angel in the flesh. Somehow we were able to successfully communicate our circumstance to him using a combination of hand signals, his Creole, and my high school French. I shared that we were in trouble, without money, family, or friends, and therefore with no place for shelter. He bought us a meal of groundnut soup and rice, and afterward took us into his nearby apartment in the Abidjan ghetto. He was a husband and a father with two small children. Kwesi and I spent the night, despite our protests and outcries, in his and his wife's bedroom. They slept on a cot and the children in a small bed.

The next day, this angel of a man walked us to the port, where we spent hours walking the shipyard for clues—the flag of a friendly nation on a docked ship, a sign of other route options by an obliging soul, or someone who would stow us away, allowing us to continue our voyage by sea. The walk on the pier and the scouring of the loading docks produced no new plans. Soon, we said our goodbyes to the kind man and were on yet another lorry, headed toward another new border. I thought about how I had traveled through three West African nations in these last few months. Kwesi had one more, Senegal, under his belt. Now, as we departed Abidjan, we were lumbering on the rutted, dust-filled roads headed toward a country I never wanted to visit, the Republic of Liberia.

•

In West Africa, traversing the outer stretches of the Niger River valley, virtually each day without exception, and nearly every experience I had, was one of revelation and wondrous discovery. Liberia was no exception.

Prior to arriving in Liberia, I held a general image of a tainted and corrupt country. In my mind, the former enslaved people who founded Liberia were handpicked Uncle Toms working in concert with slave-owning interests to thwart the abolitionist movement and to put forth a diversionary feint for a "back to Africa" movement. These "Toms" were given power and backing to divide and defeat the indigenous peoples and set up a carbon-copy regime of the United States. Liberia's flag was even red, white, and blue, a replica of the Stars and Stripes. Liberia was also one of the few places in the world, let alone of African nations, where the US dollar was the official currency. The thought of Liberia being a haven for revolutionary fugitives was absurd to me. It was, most assuredly, the last place in Africa Kwesi and I should be seeking refuge.

Little did I know that my time in Liberia would teach me some of life's most affirming and invaluable lessons. In the weeks ahead, Liberia would teach me to mobilize my body to ward off sickness, to extend love and respect, and to suspend my judgment of people. In Liberia, I would learn the power of moral might in the face of cold-blooded power; that two people, with heated and radically opposed personal views and differences, could indeed work through them, without violence or evasion. Liberia would teach me the existence of African science and spirituality. I would learn (from an extreme sense of disappointment) that it is not necessarily a bad thing if your ship does not come in as you hoped or dreamed it would. I would learn that people will more likely give you liquor to drink before they will offer you food to eat. I learned in Liberia (from the pagan masses there) that despite the overwhelming wealth mobilized to manipulate thinking and behaviors, especially through the missionaries' billion-dollar conversion enterprises there, these never penetrated beyond the most surface level the inherent customs of the people. In Liberia, I learned that if medicine's best experts were stuck, the Juju man was not. In Liberia, when lightning played its terrible dance upon the iron-laden earth, the people called on Shango.

•

We met in Monrovia. I came to know her as "Maw Mary." We quickly learned that she was Maw Mary to many. She was a strange, wonderful mix: owning a rough, no-nonsense exterior, but kind and loving interior. By Liberian standards, she was a very dark, tall woman of heavy build. Maw Mary spoke several tongues, including Ga (her principal idiom) and English. Once she knew Kwesi and me better, she would tell us, "You no go home to America. Stay here. This is your home now." She was an enigma: a deeply religious person who sold marijuana to survive and a village elder statesman, without portfolio. Though I am not certain how we met, from our very first moments in Monrovia she became a fixture in our lives.

It seemed we had always known her. My hunch is that Kwesi "discovered" her on one of his many forays to buy pot. He brought me by her house and introduced us. I took her aloofness and clipped tone as signals that she disliked me. I quickly learned she was observing, seemingly preoccupied with the stove, sifting through rice, or cleaning greens, but fully attentive to learning who we were and our relationship to each other. Her kitchen was an outdoor fireplace. In the beginning, we paid her for a wonderful meal after buying some smoke and sitting there conversing. But after several visits, we became Maw Mary's two new adopted sons.

Soon, we struck a deal with her: if we would buy food, she would prepare it. We often took her shopping to the Western-style supermarket and learned she had never been inside. The merchandise, variety of goods, and prices flabbergasted her. With the few dollars Kwesi and I received from home, we bought enough groceries for her family members and ourselves. She would feed us one meal every day in her one-room hut.

One day, we stumbled upon another deal with Maw Mary, who kept a major (if not total) portion of her grass in a shoebox. We had observed her many times, sitting with the shoebox on her lap, as she divided the grass into equal parcels to sell for a quarter. A quarter's worth was nearly a matchbox full. In Liberia, a strip of newspaper contained the parcel and served as the rolling paper for the joint. It was one big cigar-size joint for a quarter! For we Americans, this was a giant bargain, as we were accustomed to the paper-thin joints that cost at least one dollar.

Kwesi asked Maw Mary for the remnants of the weed from her shoebox. "No more—it's finished," she replied, and looked at him and then at the box. It appeared that there were only seeds and a few traces of weed left in there, so she handed the box to Kwesi. By the time Kwesi had scraped the box using a small piece of cardboard, he had uncovered about four parcels worth of pot. He lifted the edges of the box, plowed under the flaps, and proceeded to roll this unexpected surplus into several joints. It was a show of American efficiency and Maw Mary was amazed at the discarded, previously overlooked profits. With this, Kwesi became her business advisor and merited a free parcel every now and then.

Maw Mary, on a rare occasion, would say to us, "God come tonight," meaning we were welcome to visit and eat that day as usual, but that night was her night to be alone. As we finished our meal, she would sweep out her hut, light candles and incense, and spread her best blankets over her bed. We dared not challenge or question her, but simply abided by her command and left for home hours earlier than usual, to leave her alone in peace to be with God.

I credit Maw Mary with saving my life. While in Liberia, I came down with malaria. This could not have surprised me, since Kwesi and I never took any anti-malarial medicine, as the official brochures and health notices strongly advised. In our youthful pride and ignorance, we believed that sort of advice was only relevant to white folks and Europeans, not to Africa's descendants. In fact, we never saw any Ghanaians, Liberians, Malians, or Senegalese taking this medication. Our Pan-Africanist mentality forced us to ignore science as "white lies." Little did we know Africans were dying of malaria across the continent and by the thousands every day.

At first, I had no idea I had contracted malaria. All I knew is that I felt horrible. On one of his regular visits to Maw Mary, Kwesi casually told her I was too ill to leave the YMCA where we had been staying. (Finding a Y in Liberia offered a surprising reminder of home.) She demanded that he bring me to her house. Somehow, he half-walked, half-dragged me to her hut. I was weak, burning up from fever, and floating in and out of consciousness. I was in terrible shape. I remember being placed in her bed, stripped of all my clothes, and soaked repeatedly from head to toe in alcohol.

I received glimpses of my treatments as I drifted between sleep, delirium, and wakefulness—the smell of incense burning, a mosquito net draped over the bed, mournful chanting. It was a kind of war chant, a stirring call to do battle. In fact, the most vivid recollection I have during this sickness with malaria is of the dream I had while lying in her bed: I saw and felt hands twisting my spine. Two colorless, near transparent hands, much like the hands of a baseball player gripping a bat, twisting, twisting, and tightening. I felt the presence of an adversary, a force trying to defeat me, but I was defiant, at war now with this nefarious force. I was no longer passively lying in bed grasping for breath and feeling miserable. No, I was fighting back. My mind and my spirit were actively engaged in battle, mobilizing energy to the frontlines. It seemed as though something simultaneously died and birthed inside of me.

A few days later, I was up, moving about, a little thinner perhaps but feeling like a conqueror, one with a mighty army and the strongest of allies. Maw Mary was the commander in chief of that mighty army.

Maw Mary was an important member of her neighborhood, respected and sought out as wise counsel. People came to her to settle disputes and to arbitrate problems, whether it was a problem between friends, something arising out of business dealings, or a couple's relationship. Once, I asked her about what seemed to be a ferocious argument between a man and a woman with lots of shouting and yelling back and forth. I did not know what the fight was about; perhaps it was a quarrel between two lovers, or a husband and wife. Through it all, Maw Mary sat and sometimes paced between them, injecting her own comments in their Ga language, and even making clucking noises from between her teeth. Then she would render her decision, a calm resolution, and the two parties would then accept the verdict and walk away in resignation.

She patiently answered my questions without looking up from her boiling pot of rice that was cooking over the open fire, stating flatly that it was "palaver." She said if the couple got their grievances completely out in the open and continued their hot debate without either walking away or striking the other person, then all else was fair and their conflict could be resolved.

·

One night, I met a young Ga woman named Coco in a club near the center of Monrovia. She was a prostitute and a special case, as she worked not the streets but a small clique of clubs that catered to European tourists and business professionals. After that first night together, we became an odd couple. She knew I was lost and wanted to help me, even though she had no real concept of what I was lost to or what I was looking for. Neither did I, exactly. There were all manner of choices available for me to turn to, but my crazily combined sense of discipline, guilt, romance, pride, and imagined personal powers were blinding.

Coco had grown up on the tough streets of Monrovia and I found her to be resilient, loyal, loving, and intelligent. Early in life, she learned what she had to do, so she did it and she did it well. Her strength was in her quick charm and mastery of situations. Beneath years and years of abiding amid hopelessness, she kept small dreams alive. Underneath layers of abuse, exploitation, physical damage, and harm, she harbored a love and dignity of self. Beneath appearances, she was a work of art, of human possibilities in a world of cruel, narrow, preemptive choices.

We claimed each other, me as her man and she as my woman. Whenever we could, we were that to each other. More often than I dared dream, we were not that to each other. She was someone else's woman for an hour, a night, or a weekend. We fought often—or at least I fought her while she weathered my verbal attacks with patience, understanding, and love. I fought my personal insecurities and often projected them onto her. Yet she saw herself as free as one can be in a world ruled by commodities: the human marketplace and the color line. She knew the score, the options before her, and played her hand.

Coco offered me her guidance like a cane to a sleepwalker, and she became my eyes and ears without ever giving me a single clue that she was, in fact, my eyes and my ears, without which I would go bumping into walls, eternally tripping over my own feet. More than anything, we became the closest of friends. She helped me grow to see that there was something inside her that the world could not corrupt or destroy. I hope I showed her there was someone in the world who would not inflict physical harm upon her or fail to recognize the royal dignity she possessed.

Coco amazed me! She often joined Kwesi and me at Maw Mary's for a big meal and preferred to only take the bones of the chicken we ate, refusing our offers of thighs, breasts, and wings. She would proclaim that those bones were the better parts of the chicken to her and most Liberians. I fell for that and realized so much later that she ate the chicken bones, or sometimes the feet or the necks, because she wanted me to eat well and be satisfied. Kindness, generosity, and love overflowed from her every single act, touch, or gesture during our short time together.

Eventually, my ego could not accept her profession and the routine rental of her body, even though I could not provide for myself, let alone for her. I would fume and fuss—dramatizing the jealousy and anger I felt—while she went away to work each night. Yet I would welcome her back the next day. She always remained calm and once again helped me recognize the reality of our relationship: she was free, but her body was not.

CHAPTER ELEVEN

BEING IN EXILE IN AFRICA was a turning point as far as my spiritual growth. We were alone with virtually no resources, but miracles, lessons, and blessings always manifested. Always. While in Ghana, the Christmas season arrived, and I was very depressed. On Christmas Eve, I was sitting on the curb, feeling particularly hopeless, when this Muslim boy sat down nearby and began saying a prayer. It opened me up, revealed a power to me. There were so many angels, from the Irishman to Maw Mary and countless strangers who helped us along the way. They led the way daily. While in exile, I learned to be more open to and more aware of invisible hands at work. Moment to moment.

After some eight months traversing the Niger River valley, the reality finally struck like a lightning bolt: *it was time to go home.* Kwesi and I were convinced. We were reading about the war and the growing anti-war movement. We learned of the mass arrests and deaths of many of our comrades back home. They were Panthers, Native Americans, students at Kent State, and the brothers in Attica. The most personal losses were the deaths of "Che" Payne and Ralph Featherstone. According to the news reports, the men were blown to bits in an explosion, dynamited in a car they were driving. The articles were written to make sport of their deaths: the quotes from the FBI and the forensic experts, more of humiliating intended conjecture than fact, portrayed the two as bumbling "wannabe revolutionaries" who had blown themselves up while transporting dynamite to an intended target. Since their lower torsos were barely recognizable, the article described them as sitting over the dynamite when it ignited.

This news served notice to us. It was, in fact, a double notice. Not only were things picking up steam at home with presidential elections on the horizon, but there also seemed to be the bleeding together of what had been mostly separate, autonomous struggles and a growing consciousness that bordered on a great swing, a shift in the public mindset. What we were sensing now in Liberia was a growing detachment, a widening alienation from the struggles. What we had once been able to dismiss easily, to let slide from our thoughts, was a sense of historical, cultural, and personally emotional distinctions and gaps between us and our African brothers and sisters. It was time to go home, regroup, reconnect, to rejoin the movement and continue our activist work from within.

I turned for help from a newfound friend, Rev. John, pastor of the First Baptist Church of Liberia, who understood our general plight, and often ministered to us with food, housing, and moral support. During our time in Monrovia, he proved to be a brave, forthright man. We met the Louisville, Kentucky, native as a referral from the director of the Monrovia YMCA. It took no time for us to feel the utmost respect for the reverend, as he was without airs or pretenses about his position or authority.

Rev. John had remained a humble servant and had not fallen victim to the corruption that often defined Liberia. Proof of his character came weeks earlier when I observed his interaction with the US Secretary of State William Rogers on a visit to Monrovia. After welcoming Secretary Rogers to his packed church, Rev. John turned over the rostrum to him. Following Rogers' humdrum speech, the good reverend rose to take his place at the rostrum. He was eloquent and daring, and literally spoke truth to power. Using the Bible, Rev. John invoked the story of David and Goliath. He not so much equated Liberia to David but rather suggested that David was all the little anti-imperialist countries of the world.

It was no question, however, as to who Goliath was. As the Bible showed, one day the small and weak would and could defeat the big and powerful. "Might does not make right," he declared. With that, Secretary Rogers turned the brightest shade of red and quickly exited stage right.

Rev. John responded to our newest pleas for help to return to America. Because of our low funds and our fugitive statuses, our travel options were highly limited. With the Biafran War waging full force in Nigeria, travel by land to Tanzania was still unrealistic. Entering the United States was also problematic for us. By land, sea, or air? Directly or indirectly, traveling to another country before finally heading home? There was a kaleidoscope of choices, each leading to more choices. We decided to put our energies into traveling by sea directly back home.

Rev. John promised to get Kwesi and me on some cargo ship bound for the New York harbor. We later learned that the ship would be flying an Israeli flag. The hitch was that we would know of the ship's arrival in Monrovia's port only minutes before it arrived and a couple of hours before it would depart for New York, as its entry was to be virtually unannounced and unscheduled. The plan was we could travel on the ship, with Rev. John footing the bill for a couple of bunk beds and chow for what would be five to seven days at sea. We were desperate, and though wary about being under an Israeli flag, we decided to go for it.

It was late morning when we got the news: the ship was coming to the port that afternoon. We had been packed for days. I could not find Coco. We tried to kiss Maw Mary goodbye, but she pushed us away saying, "Go now." She was not up for any mushy stuff.

The reverend drove us to the docks. He waited with us as we saw the ship pulling in. It appeared to be little more than a light cruiser of some sort. I wondered about the cargo. Would it be electronics, or maybe special communication devices? Surely not the tons of raw resources, heavy materials, or equipment and supplies that we had imagined. Rev. John went to the ship alone to speak to its captain. We waited anxiously near his car. He returned in a rush with a scowl on his face stating we needed shot records to reflect yellow fever immunizations. If not, the ship and crew would be quarantined for days in the New York harbor. He promised to take care of it and drove back to town to get the proper stamps and signatures.

Kwesi and I waited and waited. The sun began to sink into the sea. We paced for a long time then walked closer to the ship. The crew began to stir more deliberately, readying the ship for departure, and then the ship's motor rumbled. The last crew member went aboard, and the loading ramp was lifted. The boat began moving and we shouted, "Hey, wait a minute, we're coming aboard!" The ship slowly moved away, separating itself from the wharf and from us. We turned to see Rev's car finally entering the harbor. I screamed at the ship, tears rolling down my cheeks. I threw my baggage in the air, took off my shirt and waved it at the ship's fading silhouette. By the time Rev. John got out of the car and handed us the documents, the ship was gone, swallowed by the waves and the horizon. I sat on the ground, my hand over my face. Rev. John sighed deeply, saying. "Don't worry. There's still another way."

During this time, Kwesi and I reconnected with a Monrovian we'd met weeks earlier, Lil' JJ. I am not certain how it was we first came to meet him. He was an alert brother, wise, well beyond his twenty-something years. Perhaps he was an "accident," someone we met in one of the cafes, or someone Maw Mary introduced to us, someone we met through our comings and goings at the Y, on the streets, or through Coco, or the reverend. Who really knows? Who really cares, when our waking moments, our daily existence, was about seeking friends, winning trust, and trying to move as quickly as possible into the fabric of Monrovian life? Kwesi and I were fish out of water frantically trying to flop back in, to submerge within the only element that could sustain us—the Liberian community. Sticking out, disconnected, being naïve to our environment or without true friends was certain death, imprisonment, or some other victimization inflicted by the fittest on the weak. The antidote, the only way to survive, was to be surrounded in a cocoon of arms, eyes, minds, and mouths, to multiply by subtraction, and to become less by submerging into the whole. The Rev. John and the YMCA administrators were our most superficial layers of protection and subsistence. For true survival, to really gain strength during our time in Africa, we needed to connect to "the people."

For several weeks, maybe even months, after meeting Lil' JJ, breaking bread, conversing, and smoking pot together, we failed to see him. We did not miss him in the sense of wondering what had happened or feeling alarm or some sense of mystery. It was the nature of the city, an aspect of urban Liberian living that people came and went, disappearing and reappearing, in ebb and flow, much like West Africa's ocean tides. When he reappeared, it was just days before Rev. John's planned departure for Kwesi and me; this time he intended for us to return to America via airplane.

Lil' JJ had an amazing story to share. Weeks earlier, he was hit by a car, struck down on the streets while walking. He was transported to the local hospital, unconscious, with serious damage to his head and body. After some time in the hospital, the doctors reported to his family that they could do nothing and that he was going to die. Undaunted by the medical report, his family removed him from the hospital, carried him to the bush, and turned him over to the "African scientists," or Juju men.

Kwesi and I had heard stories, even read articles in the mainstream local press, tales of peculiar kinds of "accidental" deaths, people being shrunk to doll size, people mysteriously struck by lightning, trees inexplicably falling on people, killing them. There were tales and reports of curses, spells, and eerie sightings. A Liberian lightning storm was a different phenomenon than what we had ever experienced in the States or anywhere else in the world for that matter. Due to the rich accumulation and abundant concentration of iron ore in the Liberian earth, lightning behaved in unusual ways. In Liberia, it was common for lightning to roll along the ground for hundreds of feet, as if in an electronic dance.

Legend has it that, especially in the bush, you would have to get under your bed during a lightning storm and cover your eyes. There would be a Juju man, a patron of Shango, the deity of war and lightning, who would dance along the streets during such a storm. He was a person with the power to direct the lightning bolt wherever he chose. If you were so defiant as to cast your eyes upon the man, you were subject to being struck by a bolt.

As we sat with him the night before our pending departure, Lil' JJ must have felt our anxiety, unease, and evasiveness to questions about what we were planning to do next. We wondered aloud, telling him we were heading to possible arrest back home. He told us not to worry, but to meet him in the next few nights and he would find us protection.

We met him at the home of one of his relatives, in a room lit only by three candles. We sat on the floor, Kwesi and I facing him, forming a triangle with a large bowl of water in the middle. He spoke in a voice just above a whisper. He spoke in his own tongue. Though we did not understand a single word of what he spoke, we were quiet, still, and attentive. He gathered some tiny pebbles in his hand and began to speak to us in English. He told us that at that moment we were like those pebbles. He let them slide between his fingers into the bowl of water. The pebbles scattered and floated to the bottom; tiny ripples quickly emerged and faded. Those tiny little bubbles, within a flash were there, then gone. He then reached for and clutched a larger stone in his hand. He told us it was many pebbles formed into one. He let it go, dropping it into the water.

Solid rings of water, concentric circles, formed, venturing out in equal symmetry around the stone and becoming absorbed against the sides of the bowl. He chanted, made offerings to the Ancestors. He communicated to those spirits, and he wanted us to know that a way had been prepared for us to arrive in New York, to walk through customs, through all the security as if we were invisible. We only had to be in accord with one another. Our unity made us like what the stone produced: a full circle emanating from the stone; a wave of protection that allowed nothing to penetrate us. As long as we held onto that unity, we would be safe and free.

Lil' JJ had never been to the United States and yet he recognized it as the "belly of the beast." He knew our strength and power was in unity. It was all that was ever needed to defeat an empire. I left immersed in a newfound belief and knowing that our pending steps were the right ones, and that we would continue to be protected on our journey.

A few days later, Kwesi and I flew nonstop from Monrovia to New York, walked through customs and security at JFK International Airport, and safely exited onto the chilly streets of New York City. The reverend had made good on his promise. Now it was time for me to make good on mine: to rejoin the movement and work for peace and justice.

•

Manhattan's air was forty degrees colder than Liberia's. Our thin African dashikis did little to protect Kwesi and me from the chilly, nipping winds. We had a few dollars in our pockets, Canadian passports in our bags, and some old, untested phone numbers and addresses of friends, relatives, and comrades in the Big Apple. Thus, we began our reentry into the United States of America.

We woke up a few folks during the late-night hours, rang apartment buzzers of one or two people we trusted. Within seventy-two hours, we managed to obtain food to eat, warmer clothing to wear, and money for Greyhound bus tickets. We began a new trail, taking an hour at a time, one mile at a time, and headed west through the Northeast's industrial "Brown Belt." We found refuge in Cleveland, in Toledo, and settled for a few nights in Detroit. We were refueled by conductors, stationmasters, and innkeepers of a modern underground railway. Countless and nameless individuals became our angels of grace and mercy, alongside near and dear relatives and cohorts. Folks, Black, Brown, red and white; humans of the cloth, the mask, the rogue, the blue collar, the white collar, and no-collar, gave us refuge, hope, and a bridge to the next station on our perilous, noble journey.

We hit Chicago and plunged into its South Side. It took nearly two years (from June 1969 to June 1971), but after journeying over 25,000 miles during that span of time, here I was, only a thousand miles from where the journey began; in the same time zone and just three states north of Texas. Despite being on US soil, standing smack dab in the middle of this predominantly Black community, surrounded by familiar aromas, sounds, and sights, everything seemed foreign to me.

It was I. I was foreign. I was not the same person who, two dozen months earlier, jumped on an airplane bound for that weekend trip to Connecticut, and wound up across the ocean in a lorry in the West African bush. Nor was I the person who lived for seemingly endless months in a Greek neighborhood in Montreal, or who rode in a taxi with the meter turned off, being rescued by a revolutionary cabbie. I was not that person who sat on a rocky beachside throne on the eastern coast of Nova Scotia feeling the soothing power of mescaline pumping through his veins, or the man who sat feeling dejected, hungry, and thoroughly lost in Bamako, Mali, as menacing vultures circled above. Nor was I the same man who could relax, laugh, and joke; sleep through the entire night without springing to his feet, gun in hand, ears searching for confirmation of intruders.

I was so close to home, yet so far removed. I truly felt like a visitor, a reluctant tourist. I was a desperate man, seeking to transplant a life onto fresh soil.

Those we had met or re-met prior to arriving in Chi-Town were graciously armed with new referrals, tips, phone numbers, and addresses to a handful of citizens and allies of liberation. It was there in Chicago that we were finally able to rest a while. The Windy City became our temporary home base. But Kwesi would grow restless and, for the first time in over a year, we went separate ways.

CHAPTER TWELVE

IT WAS IN MY 1970 sanctuary of the South Side of Chicago, Gangster Disciples gang territory, that I first saw her. She was standing in the apartment's courtyard talking to several people gathered around. I had stumbled there, emerging from my third-floor apartment for a breath of fresh air after spending afternoon hours painting barren walls. I stood unnoticed, about thirty feet away. She wore faded blue jeans, cut into shorts, and a gold Ban-Lon blouse. The sleeveless blouse helped emphasize her slender brown arms. Her hands gestured as she spoke, telegraphing her points to rapt listeners. I stood at the edge of the steps watching, debating whether to join them or not. Though I had never seen her before, I knew then that she must be Carmen Vernardo.

Months before ever seeing her, I had heard of her. Everyone in the complex seemed to know her and admire her in some way. During my short stay, no week would pass without some references to her, utterances of her name. During my very first weeks of living in these apartments, she was in Cuba cutting sugar cane and "witnessing socialism in practice." I was curious. I would often hear people asking if there was any news of her. It was after I heard someone shouting, "Carmen's back!" that I stood in the courtyard seeing her for the first time. I was so flustered that I decided not to meet her then, not like that. A basketball rolled to my feet, and I picked it up. Some kids ran over yelling for me to throw it back. Teasing them, I dribbled the ball, making them chase me, scream-ing, cursing, and laughing, to the park behind the apartments.

It would be useless to try to classify Carmen; she was not a type. The apartment complex itself was the center for an unbelievably wide array of souls. Carmen was the richest and the most peculiar of all souls. It did not take me long to discover that in this tiny world of 62nd and Ellis, she was recognized as poet laureate, spiritual advisor, ideologist, and witch.

There was a very loose clique of regulars in the complex, an assort-ment of students, workers, and "lumpens." There was George, an ex-con and now dean at Central College; Silva, the grass dealer; Carolyn, a social worker educated by Saul Alinsky; Sol, the young worker, forever fighting the merry-go-round of layoffs and new jobs; "Pretty Dan," the hustler; Karen, the divorcée, owner of a master's degree, welfare card, and a hysterical young son; Les, the junkie musician; Richard, the high school teacher; Anita, the waitress working her way to Africa; Robert, the steelworker; Barbara, part-time nurse, part-time jet engine mechanic; and Georgia, the Black Panther sister. George was the "old man" of the group, not simply because of his age of fifty-four years, but for his worldli-ness and drive. Next to George, Carmen was the most magnetic and ubiq-uitous citizen in the Chicago complex.

I finally met her that evening over at Carolyn's apartment, at what could be called a party. It was an unannounced occasion—it just rather hap-pened—a dozen of the community folk gathering to welcome Carmen back home. I was very enlivened, and mainly by her presence. I studied her as she described Cuba and her experiences there. She had an effortless man-ner in speaking. It was so easy to listen to her. It was a call-and-response energy. The entire room participated in her new, strange experiences. She moved us from an atmosphere of near spiritual communion to hot debate and from light talk to earth-shaking bombardments. I suspected then that nothing nearly as exquisite could be without her presence.

Later, I realized only a few remained in the room. Then Karen departed, after promising some guy a treat for walking her home. Carolyn and Georgia ducked into the bedroom, leaving Carmen and me alone. She stayed and we talked . . .

The morning light found us together at the kitchen table drunk on hot tea. It had been a marathon, a seminar of the sort that lifts barriers and lays souls bare. That night and early morning, I learned the difference between speaking *to* another and speaking *with* another. Carmen required intimacy in her life—she seemed to gasp for it as a fish out of water. It was a near-desperate need—her strength, and an essential force. I was amazed but wondered how she could not help but exhaust herself in the manner of a meteor or a prairie fire. We slept together that early morning and ran through the park in the evening.

Carmen spent her childhood in Gary, Indiana, a steel town just south of Chicago. She was the oldest of five, with three brothers and a sister. She discovered at the age of eleven, late one night, that her mother was a lesbian. For several years afterward, she ran and screamed within herself. She became an introvert in her formative years, spending time alone with books, microscopes, and collections of all sorts. She took watches, clocks, and molecules apart and reassembled them while her peers dated and played at being popular. Her solitude was her refuge. She must have appeared dull and dry to cheerleaders and football stars, yet her internal universe was aglow and exciting. Her spirit could not help but emerge, break to the surface one day, too mighty to be contained, and it did.

She became a sensitive sister, a liberated woman, and a child of the ghetto, an inventive person, an iconoclast, selfless lover, and my steadfast friend. Carmen lived her convictions, her faith. She was a wonderful inconsistency: a socialist who hoarded privacy, one who protested injustices and refused to serve on juries. She believed in people but hated laws and rules for people. She loved to dance, breaking out into a step anywhere and anytime, but dodged dance halls and ballroom floors. Carmen despised role-playing: she felt teachers should be life students as well, that parents should be at ease enough with themselves to play hopscotch or marbles with their children.

116

Once, she told me that the concept of masculinity and the defined roles for men were warped. The so-called strong, silent type, for an example, was more a frailty. To Carmen, everyone was, after all, people. There were no gods or awe-inspiring, larger-than-life heroes. I learned from a friend who made the trip to Cuba with her that she once walked up to Fidel Castro, who was visiting the American Venceremos Brigade, patted his stomach, and told him he was getting fat. The visiting Americans, along with the Cuban bodyguards and entourage, grew tense and embarrassed, but Fidel and Carmen laughed.

Chicago's 'L' trains are often only a few feet away from some apartments on the South Side. They create great vibrations, tremors, and noises at regular intervals. Somehow, people learn to adjust to and cope with the noise. One afternoon, Carmen and I were escorting a friend returning home from the hospital with her brand-new baby girl for the first time. The friend lived in one of those places where you can reach out the window and practically touch the 'L' tracks. Suddenly, a train roared by and the sleeping child awoke, flailing her arms and screaming. The baby shrieked and trembled for several long, excruciating minutes.

We were afraid for the child, who seemed tortured to the point of near convulsions. Mercifully, the train moved on, the noise subsided, and the baby eased into some calmness. As we began to leave, I said to the new mother and to Carmen that the child would soon get used to it. Carmen exploded angrily at me, saying, "You never get used to it, never!"

She continued, "Somewhere, in each of us, is the same shivering mind. It is buried deep, and we may walk around like zombies, but inside, our minds are screaming. We're all ready to stampede!"

I met Carmen at a critical juncture in both of our lives. I was on the run from the FBI and she was on the rebound from a marriage fiasco. In fact, she was still legally married, having not bothered with the courts for an official divorce decree. Her "husband" was a newly ordained Baptist preacher, a "reformed homosexual" he told her. I believed she married to resolve the social pressures on her, to satisfy her mother's wishes. I am guessing, too, that he was trying to deter his own social pressures. It did not last very long. A couple of months after the wedding, she came home early to find him in bed with another man. The marriage was over.

Despite this, Carmen was not a man-hater, nor a castrator of men. She was super feminine without being helpless or dependent. By average standards, she wasn't even that attractive. She had an asymmetrical face: very full lips and a prominent nose on a keen face. She wore her hair in a close-cropped 'fro. She had tiny breasts and long legs. Her hips were wide on her tall, thin frame. She had delicate, artsy hands and sexy eyes. I believed her when she told me that no man had ever brought her to the point of orgasm before me. (There was a rumor floating around Chicago that all the hip women told their mates this to encourage heroic efforts in bed.) At any rate, there is no loser in such a situation when self-satisfaction relies a lot on mutual satisfaction.

Carmen could go a week at a time without eating, only drinking tea and living on her "nervous energy." She described these fasts as mind stimulating. During these periods, she was most likely to engage in rituals and perform some mysterious feats. I laughed when she first told me that she could extinguish the light of a candle with her mind. One night, several of us in the apartment complex sat in a candle-lit room listening to soft music and conversing to one another when she announced she was in the proper frame of mind to show us, to reveal this energy. Someone closed the windows and placed a lighted candle directly across from her. We gathered around the floor in a small circle. She closed her eyes, and when she opened them, the candle flickered out.

•

I long understood that my stay in Chicago was a temporary one, set to be short-lived. Although I was not emotionally prepared to move on, I knew there would be a new destination, an assignment based on movement needs and priorities best suited for my own skills and experiences.

I knew that I needed IDs that would withstand being pulled over by law enforcement or scrutinized by a potential employer. Work to acquire those papers was underway, and I expected to have a new name and birthplace any moment.

Carmen knew there was more to my presence in Chicago than to simply pop up in their lives for no reason and then disappear. A well-known community leader, a force in the Chicago church, had prepared the way for me to live among them. They all felt comfortable enough with those prearrangements to accept me without prying questions and with a sense of diligence for overall security and well-being for this emerging commune.

The day came—actually it was at night—when my new documents arrived revealing my next destination. I was relieved that I would be heading to Gary, Indiana, the nearby steel town. I was to work in the community, linking the forces within the US Steel plant with the oppression within the community itself. The current struggle in Gary was that schools were closing because the school system there had insufficient resources to sustain its operations. US Steel had never been required to pay anywhere near its fair share of taxes and, as a direct consequence, there were no adequate funds to sustain the public schools.

CHAPTER THIRTEEN

AFTER SPENDING A FEW MONTHS in Indiana organizing among steel workers, I was back on the move, still without Kwesi. It was wintertime on the East Coast, Washington, D.C., late 1970. Falling raindrops were quickly becoming ice, sleet, and snow flurries. Traveling solo on new and beaten pathways led me to a routine of consciously performing on an invisible stage, striving to adapt to this new fugitive reality deep in the heart of occupied Babylon. My front became a near flat demeanor that betrayed my volatile, pins-and-needles insides. Even old, trodden pathways seemed new. I had a new take on everything in sight. Is this person checking me out, following me? Did the words I just hear, even a distant off-hand remark or the tone or phrase by a stranger, reflect or enforce a gnawing gut suspicion? I began questioning my questions, calibrating and recalibrating the micro and the macro as I moved. My body language was my only perimeter defense. Appraising and re-examining how I must appear to others: was I looking nervous? Did I mesh into the surroundings, draw unwanted attention?

I pulled over in a sprawling park in the nation's capital to get a few winks before venturing into the inner city of Washington, D.C. An old white man tapping on my passenger side window awakened me. He was mumbling something I could barely discern, something about getting a ride and pointing off into some ambiguous direction. I rolled down the window and asked him if something was wrong. He may have been drinking or maybe he was just lost. I saw dollars in his shirt pocket as he was trying to tuck them in more securely. I told him to get in. He did, still gabbing about a street, town, or maybe even a planet he wanted to go to.

I cranked up the car. He smelled like a funky wet sock. I drove slowly, sized him up, and reached my hand into his shirt pocket, pulling out a wrinkled mass of ones, fives, and tens, perhaps fifty or sixty bucks. He paid no attention to what I was doing. He seemed lost in his own wandering mind. I pulled over next to a row of trees and park benches, reached over, opened his door, and with both hands and one foot, pushed him out the door, onto the ground, and drove away.

Later, I arrived at the home of Dashiki, a dear comrade, in the middle of Chocolate City's Northwest side. This gave me a short break, a chance to unwind, catch a breath, and talk through all that was racing through my mind.

I was a wanted fugitive, and though my old SNCC comrade from southwest Georgia was not a wanted man, he surely wanted to keep it that way. Allowing me into his own sanctuary was risky business for any average law-abiding person, but for him, the dangers were compounded even more so. Dashiki's home was a testimony to his own hustling lifestyle. During the daytime hours, he directed two community centers. Neither of his two employers, from all I could surmise, knew about the other. So, even his legitimate day-work routines were on the cusp of ethical conflict-of-interest issues, activities that the IRS or those respective boards of directors would have a keen interest in investigating.

Dashiki's "workday" was only a portion of his jaunt between very thin lines inside and outside of the law. In the evening to early morn, he would cut heroin into parcels to be distributed to waiting arms and noses on the street. Through the wee hours, he was also gambling in after-hours joints, shooting craps mostly. I watched his back during those times we were together; his movements were of interest to the police, other dealers/competitors, and, most likely, to potential dope-fiend vultures, knowing he was probably carrying some serious cash and drugs.

His dress code was a survival tip for me as well. If he was broke, he would dress up and look sharper than a tack. If he was holding big bucks, he would dress down as if he was slumming. It worked, too. Someone would always buy him a drink or offer him monetary investments when he looked rich. When he was dressed down, folks would tend to shy away from him.

His wife worked as a secretary in a government agency, but stayed at home while I was there, being seven to eight months pregnant with their firstborn. Turns out she was carrying twin boys, born on Christmas Day. He named the firstborn twin Kofi, as a tribute to our relationship—I was introduced to anyone he felt needed to know as "Kofi," an African name I was given in Ghana.

Dashiki also knew Kwame Touré well from those SNCC days in the South and invited him to speak to youths at one of his community centers. It was a treat, a testimony to Touré's charismatic and oratorical powers. It was simply amazing to listen to him and witness the impact Brother Touré wielded. The young men who were led by Dashiki or had simply stumbled into the community center went from a cold, nonchalant, "I don't give a damn about whatever you say, ol' man" demeanor to rapt attention. Theirs became a laser-beam focus that rose all the way to "I'm ready to make the revolution!" crescendo, in swift symphonic order.

After a while, I was pressed for cash and needed to move on to where I could become engaged with folks in the workers' movement. I thought of returning to the Midwest or regrouping in the southern sector's liberated zones of the Black Belt South, eventually heading to the West Coast, where misdirected gangs held secret potential for welding hotly contested rivalries into alliances and much-needed multinational unity. In my mind, the East Coast was a graveyard.

The route I dreamed of taking could become a living web of cohorts that would knit new contacts into new vanguard warriors, rear support teams, and eventually establish a coast-to-coast revolutionary network.

To do this, however, I needed money. I figured it would take at least a few thousand dollars in hand to sustain my own travels, fashion some new, improved communication links, and eventually free up a couple of others to join my mission. I needed to practice making my own way, creating resources, and becoming more self-reliant. It did not take long for me to decide on a course: to rob.

After mulling over various targets, I began to case several local movie theaters. I looked for inner-city or near-suburban theaters that would provide quick escape routes, close to multiple interstate highways. I also searched for venues with a high volume of theatergoers, those offering enough show times to provide for a critical mass gathered within a certain time range, enabling the most concentration of cash. I found one. Now I needed a tight crew: two others, one to drive and another to enter the theater with me ready to provide cover as I sprang into the manager's office to collect the cash.

Dashiki identified and recruited two men who agreed to do the deed. Everything was set. I checked the target cinema, visited it to determine the routines and the best times for the hit, when it would be packed, the big-ticket sales collected, and money transferred to the manager's office. I met the men, and they were game for the plan. They understood their roles and the agreed-upon time to meet. I would be the only one packing; the driver and the lookout just needed to do their bit. But I overlooked one single, crucial detail, the central piece to the puzzle, one that I never explored or factored into the equation: the simple truth of whether these men were reliable and disciplined enough to carry out the robbery. They were not.

They never showed up at our rendezvous spot. They were loyal to heroin and only did its bidding with any regularity. That day, the two junkies got the call of a shooting gallery and spent their time nodding the night away. The great heist never happened. Dashiki shook his head as I informed him about how heroin won the day, and the revolution paid the costs because of it. I did not fault him or call him out for sticking me with two junkies. He did what he had to do, and now I had to do what I had to do.

The next morning, I was on I-95 South, headed to my long-departed SNCC posts in Georgia. There was enough money in my pocket for a few tanks of gas and some grub, thanks to Dashiki, and not much else. A few days later, I found myself working in a lumber mill, alternately stripping logs and tasting sawdust. Shortly thereafter, I worked alongside migrant workers harvesting potatoes, okra, and cabbage.

I was safe for now but began to crave my family.

CHAPTER FOURTEEN

I HAD TO FIND A way to get back home to Dallas. To see my wife, my mother, sisters, and my son. I had never laid eyes on my son. My high school friend, Ben, arranged for me to sneak into the city even though I was driving a car with Canadian license plates.

It was 6:00 PM in the evening. Getting dark. I came in through the back steps of my friend's home. The plan was to have Felicia and Ohene, who was now nearly two years old, go to a movie theater. There, they would be snuck out the back of the theater to come to Ben's home, where I would be waiting. Mom and my sister Jackie met us there as well.

It was clear my son was comfortable with Mom and Jackie. As I held Ohene, his eyes darted from person to person, but he did not try to escape my arms. Looking at my son for the first time, I was amazed. It was one powerful moment, filled with joy and excitement. He was so alert. He looked at me and never cried. After a while, he laid on my chest and I held him through the remainder of our dangerous and brief yet sweet visit.

We were limited by time, as Felicia needed to return to the theater before the movie ended. We had only an hour. Sooner than I thought, Ben cued us that it was time to leave, but I did not want to go. After a fury of hugs, kisses, and tearful goodbyes, I returned my son to his mother's arms and snuck back down the stairwell. Ben's mother never knew we were even there.

•

I quickly left Dallas for Albuquerque to visit my older sister Karen and my brother-in-law Bob at the Air Force base. This was very dangerous, but I needed to see more family and I desperately needed money. I eventually returned to Georgia and Thomasville to see my dear friends, Hiram, Sandra, and Frances, drawn like a compass pointing north. I survived once again by living with (and under the protection of) them and a small circle of their relatives and friends. Things were a little different. Frances had her own place, and the matriarch of the family had passed on.

Sandra had a boyfriend. Somehow, she communicated to him that I came before him; that I was back, and he needed to stay out of the picture. His love for Sandra eclipsed his fuming abhorrence of me and he complied with her orders. During my time there, he did nothing to harm me or rid me of my freedom.

I was able to regroup in Thomasville, and after a few weeks moved on to the West Coast. I went to Compton to stay with Betty Fikes, my daughter Angie, and their family, who had moved there a couple years earlier. In Compton, I worked on an assembly line for Waste-King. When I settled in there, I sent for San, and she came without hesitation. Through the period when I was unable to move about with a sense of security or find work, San became my link to the world. She took on a job as a waitress and I was later able to secure work on an assembly line, connecting with fellow workers to build new recruits for the movement.

Another few months passed and the situation required that I move on and take on riskier tasks outside of Los Angeles. I asked Sandra to leave, to return home to Georgia. I know it was hurtful and cold in so many ways, but she left, like a soldier in an undeclared war, never questioning why. I did not realize fully then, and it was only much later that it hit me fully and squarely: no one outside of my blood family ever loved me unconditionally—and without ever failing to manifest it in word and deed—as San did.

•

I found a place to lay low in Denver, where I was reunited with an ex-con named Lafayette, who taught me how to get money by playing dumb to white people. I learned a lot from ex-cons, pimps, even gangsters while on the run. What I learned kept me alive and afloat. Lafayette was a unique man. Before he served time in prison he had women boosting clothes for him, ran all kinds of game. In prison he became a student of revolutionary change and began to reframe his life, and upon his release he moved to Dallas, connected with Dallas SNCC and became a core element to our work. He devoted his hustling assets and experiences, and intentionally used his money to help the revolution by paying for bonds and lawyer fees.

I eventually made it to Detroit, where I joined other activists to support the D.R.U.M. (the Dodge Revolutionary Union Movement) and the League of Revolutionary Workers. They were autoworkers who believed they were the ideal people to lead a revolution for decent, hardworking men and women. It was an exciting time to be among these newfound brothers and sisters.

I decided to head to Cincinnati next. But while it was still in Detroit, getting ready to board a bus at two or three in the morning, cops pulled me over. I had luggage and a box with a gun on me. Thankfully, they did not see the gun. This was yet another narrow escape for me.

Cincinnati, however, would yield a surprising end to my journey. First, Kwesi had finally rejoined me. We were busted just a few days after our arrival while en route to a job interview with the Office of Economic Opportunity, an organization that fought the war on poverty, that was arranged by a former SNCC worker, George Hughes. A team of FBI agents, as well as uniformed and undercover police, swooped in on us from multiple directions, sealed off the car we were in. One agent held a photo of me in his hands, called my name, and pointed at me. With drawn weapons, they handcuffed us and carted us off to a cell inside the FBI office. We never saw George again. With the benefit of hindsight, it seems the man we trusted—the one who referred us and drove us to the supposed interview—was himself an undercover agent for the FBI.

While in Hamilton County Jail, we had a chance to escape. Some of the inmates planned to break out and invited us to participate. They had arranged for a visitor to put a gun in a trash can that an inmate trustee was able to retrieve. Twenty-seven inmates got out that night but found themselves back in jail two days later, as they were true criminal elements— pimps and robbers. Kwesi and I were relieved not to have gone blindly with them. A few days later, we were both headed back home to Dallas— the notorious fugitives finally captured—where we would spend time in an all-too-familiar place while we awaited trial: the Dallas County jail.

•

Upon my return to Dallas in chains, I pleaded guilty to the federal offense of failure to appear in court on the advice of my attorney, Ed Polk. They reminded me that I could not prove innocence or be found not guilty otherwise. All the prosecutors had to do was simply ask where I was on each and every day that I was not present in court to prove I failed to appear in court. My allegations of fearing for my life, my certainty that I would be railroaded by an unjust racist system—none of it mattered. Polk assured me that the reasoning for my disappearance, regardless of the truth behind it, would fall on blind, deaf, and dumb judges and jurors.

Moreover, Polk worried that my federal sentence could be arranged in a way to cause me to serve my federal and state prison time consecutively rather than concurrently. The other federal charges—draft evasion and the firearms violation—had been dropped. But the State of Texas had reaffirmed the ten-year sentence I got from the OK Supermarkets boycott. If I fought the "failure to appear" charge and lost, I could very easily wind up spending a maximum of thirteen to fifteen years in prison versus three to ten. I succumbed to those realities and pleaded guilty, and received concurrent sentences. It was over.

First, I was allowed to read my own statement into the record:

Let me express to the court the fact that those subsequent charges once attached to this court for disposition have been dismissed. I am referring to the draft evasion and firearms violation charges. From the very beginning, your honor, I, and many within the community, were keenly aware of their highly transparent and flimsy nature. Moreover, they reflected then, as they do now, the systematic attempt to remove me, and by any and all means necessary, from the political activities that we of the Student Non-Violent Coordinating Committee were pursuing organizationally at that time. The draft charges actually stemmed from a petty and technical violation of the Armed Forces Examining and Entrance station rule of smoking in a no smoking zone! There couldn't have been any serious attempt to induct me into the Armed Forces, as I was under criminal charges by the State of Texas at the time; charges that are still under appeal in the Higher Courts. I, at no time, and it can be easily shown, indicated to those induction officers that I had any intent not to submit to induction. Their very eagerness to act and have me imprisoned preceded any actions on my part that would reflect "draft evasion" or a refusal for induction.

As a community organizer, I studied and have been sufficiently trained in the rules, regulations, and laws pertaining to the Selective Service Act. I am fully aware of my rights in relation to Selective Services. It was the very organizational activities and practices I and others were engaged in demanding recognition of those very rights for all inductees, and my volunteer counseling to others on their legal rights, that were the true cause, motivation, and a handy justification to level charges at me for draft evasion.

The firearms violation charges were also dropped. Those federal charges are indicative of the same self-styled tactics used in the draft case, to disrupt or neutralize our movement for self-determination. There was an additional and immediate objective though: to render serious bodily harm or deadly force. A pre-dawn raid was conducted on my home by more than twenty-five police agents who blocked off adjacent streets, surrounded my apartment, and broke in my door. My life and the lives of the three other occupants—my wife and another married couple sharing that two-bedroom apartment—were saved only by the alert and quick actions of my wife. The burning question remains: why were the DPD, FBI, DPS, and ATF officers crashing through my home to attack us? The firearm that was used as the pretext for this home invasion was legally purchased and owned by me. The claim that I owned an illegal firearm was purposefully false. How could I have violated any laws when I purchased the rifle openly, over the counter, and outright at a department store? I was not a convicted felon as was falsely alleged, but the ploy used to cover their tracks. I was free on an appeal bond challenging the entire court process. My state felony conviction was not a final conviction as the case itself was bound for review in the Texas Court of Appeals to determine if indeed I received a fair trial in the first place.

Pure and simple, these instances were acts of systematic repression, acts of harassment and wholly illegal in the eyes of the law. They were plain and simple gestapo activities occurring daily to members of SNCC; clear evidence to us and to the general community that establishment forces were fixed on nothing less than eliminating our organization and our dynamic activities from pursuing our basic civil and human rights.

One of the stipulations for granting me release on bond in the draft evasion case was the restriction of my travels to the Northern District of Texas. Due to the nature of my work, it was necessary for me to travel outside the court's stipulated area. An agreement was reached between my court appointed attorney and the US Attorneys allowing me permission to travel. In each instance of travel, an established procedure for traveling outside of North Texas came into effect. It required my attorney to inform the US Attorney of the proposed trip, providing the purpose of the trip, the destination's address and phone numbers, and the amount of time away. In each and every instance, this procedure was followed precisely.

On June 28, 1969, I was to address the National Council of Churches at a conference in Greenwich, Connecticut, and was advised by my attorney that I was able to attend as the standard procedure were followed, as in all previous travels outside of Texas. It was only upon my arrival in Greenwich that I learned by telephone from my court-appointed attorney, Mr. Don P. Wills, that an arrest warrant had been issued for my arrest for leaving Texas, and that I could be arrested at any moment for violating the travel agreement. I asked him to explain how I had violated the bond since he himself contacted the US Attorney utilizing the same process as had been established in all prior travels I undertook outside the District's boundaries. He responded by saying that they never formally agreed for me to travel and his advice for me to travel to Connecticut was premature.

It was clear then to me that I had been duped in a set-up. My attorney then advised me to "sneak back" into Dallas; not to use any public transportation because the FBI and other law enforcement agencies were most likely monitoring the airports, train stations and bus terminals. Now, because I was facing new and additional trumped-up charges, imminent arrest or worse was in store. It appeared that I had become, in the eyes of police at least, a justifiable target for deadly force. I felt in fear for my life, I decided then and there to opt for survival, and that remaining free was in my best interest. I felt that my only recourse was to withdraw, to retreat from direct and possibly deadly attacks. I ran for my life, knowing that to do otherwise, to stand as a perfect target to hostile, rampaging forces intent on violence, was suicidal.

Those lessons I'd drawn from the assassinations of Medgar Evers, Dr. King, and Malcolm X were real. The more recent shooting of Huey P. Newton by police officers; the murders of Fred Hampton and Mark Clark by agents of the US government as they slept, all was sufficient fuel for propelling me into a fight-flight for survival. The murderous deaths of dozens of Panthers that summer alone was fresh ammunition for my feelings. In Texas, Houston's SNCC leader was sentenced to thirty years in prison in a crudely arranged frame-up.

During my own trial, members of the local press testified to my attorneys that they overheard Dallas police swear they would kill me for the slightest opportunity. I even heard one jailer tell me to my face that a pine box was waiting on me at the Ellis Prison Unit. The raid on my home proved to me that the slightest pretense was provocation enough used to justify—in the eyes of the law—what would be otherwise considered unjustifiable brutalities. Therefore, within the totality of my experiences simply as a Black man, and one engaged in the work that challenged white power and racism, my life was at risk, in great danger. I knew in my heart and soul I could not receive any semblance of justice in Dallas, in America. Dallas was my birthplace, my wife's and my entire family. My leaving home was never before or then a pre-calculated act. It was a hot, spontaneous reaction to real threats by coercive, ruthless forces, nurtured, propped up, and validated within a deeply rooted good ol' buddy-buddy system. Never was it my willful intent to obstruct or evade those court proceedings to be held on July 7, 1969. Rather, it was but a natural recourse to save my life.

It would be a terrible error, and one to the greatest extent, to separate or attempt to isolate my situation today before this court from the overall, everyday plight of poor people and especially Black people, people of color. The energies and strivings that have crystalized and been leveled at me; the charges I face here and in the Texas State Courts are inseparably connected to the massive forces of oppression and exploitation that Black and Brown people, basically, all poor and working impoverished people of this city, this state, this nation, and indeed of this world, face daily.

There is a daily, systematic, backbreaking, life-stealing oppression that serves as the basis of this country's rule since its very origins. What other or more realistically accurate terminology can one honestly apply to the very fact that armed invaders swept these very shores and through the most savage acts of violence, attempted to destroy a whole race—this land's original, native inhabitants—purposefully, systematically striving to take their lives, through cannon and gun, through the spread of diseases like smallpox by the distribution of infected blankets, and through the willful and needless extermination of the buffalo, a major pillar of their economic way of life? Can we rightfully term it the "Great Expedition," as our school textbooks proclaim?

What is the rationalization one should attach to the fact that human beings, a whole continent, was raided to enslave millions? How can one accurately describe or justify the undeniable fact that whole communities were captured, stolen from their homelands, and forced under chains and lashes to toil night and day for another's pure profit? Should we say that whole African nations were obliged to do so because it was Manifest Destiny? Is that the right rhetoric one should apply to those eons of intergenerational tragedies? Can we say that a pat on the back, a jeweled trinket for twenty years of wage slavery in death filled coal mines, or the murderous, life sucking threads of assembly lines, or at the burning furnaces of coke plants, is the just reward for the so-called "decent living" we hear so much talk about? Should one believe that the murders of Dr. King, Carl and Fred Hampton, George Bess, George Jackson, and countless other men and women were the acts of isolated and individual terror? But how then should one describe the ongoing criminal persecutions of other brave souls like Lee Otis Johnson, Reies Tijerina, Paul Robeson, Fred Bell, Angela Davis, or Geronimo Pratt and others of the Black Panther Party? Are these the examples of those being the "greatest threat to the people of this country"? Is this the absurdity we are to believe?

How are we to account for the very fact that people starve every day in this nation, that millions are without even the simplest basic shelter, while a tiny handful grow fat and flabby from the spoils of corporate riches? Why is it that thousands die simply because they can't afford proper medical attention while others are able to maintain the very best in personal health care? What reasons exist that can explain the fact that every man ever put to death in gas chambers or in electric chairs are poor people whereas the rich and super rich rarely if ever serve prison time at all?

One can correctly conclude that the wealth of this nation is limited to the very privileged few; that the institutions of the state serve to maintain this relationship of exploiter and exploited; that we are in the midst and are witnessing the development of a completely fascist state, and most importantly that the only hope for change lies in the resoluteness and successful struggle of all oppressed people united in a common effort for liberation in our times.

And, with that, I was forced to give up my freedom for a time.

PART FOUR:

PRISON LETTERS TO MAMA

MY FEDERAL AND STATE SENTENCES were to run concurrently. I was to serve the federal term first, which turned out to be about one year, and then be transferred into the custody of the State of Texas to begin what turned out to be an additional two years. My first stint was in the Federal Correctional Institution Texarkana. It was a minimum-security facility where I met former accountants, elected officials, and draft evaders. It was there that I met and began a long-term connection with Walter Collins, a dedicated, highly effective organizer out of New Orleans, who had been convicted of draft evasion. Collins had been associated with SNCC as well as the Republic of New Africa, where his strong, charismatic mother served as vice president. She and my mother became close colleagues, supporting their sons and the movement in general.

But I wasn't long in Texarkana, just six or seven months before I was suddenly transferred to United States Penitentiary Leavenworth, a maximum-security prison. I sensed my quick transfer was due mainly to the work Walter and I had managed to carry out together in Texarkana—organizing political study groups and generating solidarity inside and outside of those walls in support of the Black liberation movement and against the war in Vietnam.

The sight of Leavenworth was immediately horrifying. From the prison bus, those formidable red-brick walls and gun towers were an imposing image, far more menacing than the little gates and relative openness of Texarkana. I was placed first in a four-man cell, and then another cell with seven other occupants, a mix of bank robbers, kidnappers, and drug dealers. Everyone, I found, kept within their peer cliques, where they enhanced their networks and shared among each other tricks of their respective trades, as well as the mistakes and lessons learned.

I quickly located my own peers: revolutionaries, renegades, and militant agitators of every color of the rainbow. Each sector, Red, Black, and Brown had won, through years of struggles with prison authorities and administrators, concessions to have legitimate, officially recognized clubs, or "workshops." I gravitated to the Black Cultural Workshop that had an outside sponsor—the noted historian Dr. Jacob Gordon from the University of Kansas—and the authority to bring in speakers and cultural workers as well as hold special events. We had our own newsletter, and I became a member of the editorial/publication team. In fact, the work of the BCW became my full-time occupation there. We built strong alliances with the Chicano, Puerto Rican, and Native Indian workshops. There were even a few "John Browns," white revolutionaries that allied with our common causes for prisoner rights, dignity, and justice. While the rebellion in Attica raged, prisoners around the country went on hunger strikes and mounted petition drives and letter-writing campaigns. When George Jackson and brothers in California prisons—like Folsom, San Quentin, and Soledad—were attacked, prisoners around the country protested in varying ways, wearing black armbands and the like, to demonstrate solidarity. When brothers and sisters in the American Indian Movement confronted repression, or the Young Lords protested, each of the cultural workshops strived to translate those actions into campaigns for justice within the prison walls. It appeared that Leavenworth was a driving force within the national prison rights movement.

After a year or so, I was paroled from Leavenworth, forcibly transported back to Texas, and spent the next two years respectively in the

Walls Unit, Retrieve Prison Farm, and Ramsey I. The following letters, written to my mother from April 1972 to August 1974, survived in the care of her personal archives. They reflect those times and conditions and serve as an account of the loving relationships sustaining me through hell and back.

1972

Dallas County Jail
17 April 1972

Dear Mama,

Inspirational letter! I know the future surely allows me the opportunity to try and prove worthy of your honor!

I think there is a positive force(s) at work in everything, and if we look at the other side of the coin of my present situation, we'll find many rich examples. I think struggle is not to be feared but welcomed. Just thinking of the educational aspects alone could prove my point. The unfavorable conditions help fashion us concretely; making us stronger, tightening up our family (is that possible!) and communal bonds— welding us together in a way—exposing us to the realities of life thus providing us with new meaning. In fact, life is propelled forward only through struggle.

It was primitive man's fight with nature that made possible the wheel, the lever, the ax; basic tools whose utilization by man separates him from the lower animal. There is a phenomenon in Africa, I hear, of welcoming in a way the scourge of malaria. Especially in children, for it is a test for survival. The young that survive are made stronger by the struggle with malaria.

In attempting/struggling to change a thing, we inevitably change ourselves. In struggling against forces of stagnation, the seed of the new man rises in us. It's almost an incredible happening but a real occurrence! I see clear signs of the future man in you, Jackie, Fe, Kat, Kay—that is true positivity.

Each day, all the old arguments and attempts to justify and defend this corrupt system grow more and more absurd. What was relativity new and vital in the 1700s is old and mildewed. Each day is an advance, a step forward, and we are more and more clearly aware of the superfluous nature of the Billy Grahams, Hunts, Nixons, and Agnews. Today, we see their unnecessariness (such a word?) until tomorrow it presents itself as a fetter or a hamper for all mankind. It will be unable to go forward out of its own weight and clumsiness.

Oh, I got the stamps. Didn't receive the bread that Aunt Gwen left! Beautiful thing on Don. Just got a letter from him and I'll relay the happenings. Whatever happens Thursday, the fight goes on. Even probation, as you said, is a real trick bag!

Take good care.

Your son,
EM

P.S I wear a thirty-two waist and thirty-one length in pants. But I think the ones downstairs will do for now. Have y'heard 'bout the clothes in Cincy? Careful 'bout George [*Hughes, the person who allegedly set Kwesi and me up for our arrest in Cincinnati*] for now—will fill you in!

•

Dallas County Jail
28 April 1972

Dearest Mama,

Received your letter dated Wed. morning and it sounds like things are cooking! I had an inner feeling, so I'm really surprised by the good news. Things here are 'bout the same. Maxie [*a fellow prisoner in the cell block*], for one though, is completely retrograde in his outlook and I've thrown my hands up. There are limitations—those who refuse to help themselves are out of my range of assistance. It's unfortunate that we keep moving on . . . Quinn [*another fellow prisoner in the cell block*] is grasping things but sometimes I feel it's for conversational purposes to impress. A beginning? And Jordan [*also in the cell block*], he wallows in the trivial and petty, purposefully. So much for death row. Really though, everything is cool. I feel as we all do—the beginning of a new cycle. It's uncomfortable to adjust but we manage.

Hey, I wrote Fe a serious letter. I know the last time we had such serious and frank dealings things got pretty insecure for a moment. The possibility of negative short-term pain is possible, but the long-range effect will strengthen our relationship. I know she looks to you for help, although she won't admit it. I recall the time she left a letter from me over at your place. It was one similar in tone only to the present one. Perhaps, that was her way of saying "help." I know she didn't leave it accidentally as she told me what she did with it.

Don's woman Faye [a newly discovered ally who lives in Texarkana, near to where I am to be shipped] sent me some info on the visiting situation at Texarkana. It sounds very, very good comparatively speaking! They have a courtyard where people can sit together in the yard, dig. Touch! The visiting days are Sat. and Sun (and holidays) 8:30–11:30 AM/12:30–3:30 PM. I can surely dig on the sun and touch aspects (smile).

Heard from Kelly [*a recommended attorney*] yet? After getting a clarification from Ed [*Polk, a strong ally, and my attorney during the latest court proceedings*] on his relations to the other mentioned attorneys, I went ahead and made known what my feelings and objectives were. He will take whatever action is necessary, pending further information. He seemed outraged, too (an act?). Oh well, despite my skepticism, I feel we'll get to the bottom of things yet.

Mrs. McMillan (smile) I'll close now. Yes, I got info on W. Scott. I never heard of him. How'd he get the address? Looking forward to seeing y'all Sunday.

With much love.
Yo son.

•

Federal Correctional Institution, Texarkana, Texas
16 May 1972

Hey Mama,

'scuse me for such a delay. I'm way behind in everything! I have mop duty in a few minutes and it's a long hallway, too (smile).

Things are coming along a little better now. I am still to be classified. Completed just about all the examinations and forms, etc. Took a SAT and IQ test the other day and I'm crossing my fingers in anticipation for a job that will be productive and useful on the outside! This mop and broom ain't gon' get it. I guess you can see I'm in a little better spirit than last week.

I looked for you and the "gang" over the weekend, but I realize all the problems involved, so I'm developing a more realistic outlook. Perhaps, a holiday weekend may be best, but again the traffic on the highway will be too rough for that. When fools dominate the roads, it's best to let them have it for their day.

When I left DCJ they said I had a total of $5 in property. My guess is that Jackie left it. Things were moving so fast that I couldn't adequately challenge them as to this being the correct amount.

I have your picture on the wall, so it seems that I have settled in for a while. Y'all sho' lookin' good! I've made some good acquaintances but my main man who I knew on the outside shortly is in the hold. He's a political prisoner from New Orleans and a brilliant/sharp dude. He has a helluva family; reminds me of my loves. His mother is Vice President of the Republic of New Africa and his brother visited Cuba with the work brigade. Received a beautiful note from Kathy. Writing her tonite! I'm still behind with Kay, Mildred, Gwen, Californians, but I'll write them soon . . .

Mom, you know I've never told you that you were a grandma before Ohene's birth . . . I have a daughter, seven years old this April. I guess I was ashamed of it in the past and I only related it to Jackie. Her life and presence on earth has taken on a new meaning to me in the recent past. I searched and searched and found her and she's a Partee down to the toes! Her name is Angela (and she is). She was born in Selma, Alabama, in '65. Her mother is a beautiful and strong woman. She's singing in L.A. in a nightclub now, I think. Her voice is great. She sang blues/folk music in Newport and with the SNCC "Freedom Singers." We are good friends, period. She was younger in age than I was when we met, but more mature in mind. I guess I was too wild then and she knew.

She went away from home with full knowledge of her pregnancy but refusing to "burden me" with it. I found out much later from secondary sources. Angela saw me and called me Daddy right off. Her mother's honesty and openness to her daughter is remarkable. We, Bettie and I, became the best of friends, respectful partners. Well, I could write all night about her, but I'll stop for now. I'll enclose her picture if the hack says OK. I felt the burning need to tell you for months now and I just couldn't contain it any longer. Share with me the beauty of this knowledge please.

I wrote Neva and Faye asking if they could get Buff to send me their address. I haven't heard from them since. Is this why? If so, I hope it doesn't affect you in the same way. I guess if someone accepts, they must accept all of me, not selected parts . . . If the hack says it's permissible, I'll enclose her picture for you.

Well, the mop crew is preparing for its mighty mission, so I'll close for now. I'll write later. Love to Jackie/Yiki! Take care of yourself.

Love ya' so,
Ernest

•

Federal Correctional Institute, Texarkana, Texas
22 May 1972

Hey Mama,

I found out through my liaison officer that I am finally to be classified on Wed. From that date onward, I will be doing some regular work (slave labor), probably in the hospital.

I've been talking to a lot of men from Dallas, and we've agreed on a project that we all would like to work toward seeing brought about. Basically, it amounts to the relatives and family of Dallas prisoners pooling together to share in transportation to ease the hassles and financial burden of coming out to visit. I discussed it with the chaplain's office, and they've agreed to go to bat for us to the administration. I wrote a letter to Zan yesterday, seeking to see if he could call the church (some churches) to initiate and carry out the task. I have high hopes that a regular thing could be worked out. Maybe you could talk with him and see where his head is. I was thinking of the church perhaps providing a bus (through a collective effort) and at least once a month at a predetermined place the relatives meet and use transportation to Texarkana and back to Dallas, to the central area.

If this works, I will try the same thing for men from other areas that are well represented here like New Orleans, Houston, etc. Let me know what you think about it! If it's feasible or practical? This goes for Black as well as Brown, and white families. Also, in talking with the chaplain he hit on me about Black groups coming out to entertain the men. He says they have been limited to a shaky program because there are not very many Black people in Texarkana, plus their budget is low. Maybe, the El Centro NTSU students could work out something to present or maybe that Black boxer could exhibit his talents or maybe some Black musicians or artists could come out and contribute a little time for the men?

Things here are on the dead side and there's no reason for it since the administration isn't as restrictive as say DCJ. If Zan isn't capable of coming through for us on the busing issue (smile), perhaps Rev. Saunders with the World Council of Churches, Rev. Lacy [*a progressive, stand-up pastor in South Dallas*], or Don Johnson [*a strong ally as well as a welcome critic of SNCC*] or Ed Washington [*a steadfast, grassroots community leader in South Dallas*] could be approached. I'll contact each of them one at a time if Zan doesn't come through. If they fail, I'll go national with it. Somehow, some links between prisoner and community have to be concretely fashioned. One small step at a time, huh?

I trust you are well. I received the $5 in the form of a check. They tell me it will take a month to process! I think they want to discourage anything but federal postal money orders. I have very small needs and I think $12 a month will get me by all right. At any rate, we can't spend over $25 per month. When I start work, I should be able to handle cigarette money.

Jackie's moving caught me by surprise, although it's certainly long overdue for her to "try her wings." I know that will call for some bit of adjustment, to say the least. I hope everything works out for you OK. Let me know how you feel about it, OK?

The reason I failed to see Mary G [*Mary Greene, a dear ally and former Dallas Urban League staffer, then with the Children's Television Workshop*] and Don was not because I didn't have them on my visiting list as you say, but because I'm still being classified—maximum, medium, or minimum security. I'm only allowed immediate family, for the time being.

Please tell me more about the student program that you mentioned in the letter, sounds interesting.

I love you mama and I'm working to master some skills that will be an asset to helping to provide some financial security when I'm released. It's a college chemistry course, one of my old favorites. Also entered some writings in a contest—fingers crossed.

Take care. Pardon my hectic writing spells. I think I'm finally getting my feet on the ground.

Love ya' so,
Ernest

P.S. Excuse this leaking pen too!

•

Leavenworth Federal Prison, Leavenworth, Kansas
5 June 1972

Hey Mama—Love,

Great news 'bout Angela [*Davis*], huh?!! It's strengthened a lot of hopes this way that the people can win. I would be hard pressed to think what they would have done to her if her people's support (national and international) wasn't so strong! I can only think of a young sister (Black) on death row in the Carolina's with a charge much flimsier than Angela's—and she has the death penalty. Angela's pledge to wage the unified effort to free all political prisoners is correct. There's only one Angela Davis but millions (past & present) that face the same violence she faced.

It's also great news about Ohene's nursery program! A foreign language, too? My! I'm going to have to really hone down just to talk with him. Really, it is fine news and a great relief all the way round.

No mama, the fellas here aren't blind at all! Anyway, I agree with their opinion you look beautiful and youthful—you must get away from the folks with the bad eyes in Dallas more often.

Mama I was under the impression you left some money last time, but I'm hesitant about raising cane to the authorities because I'm not sure. I was on such a trip on your visit I can't remember exactly.

Things in the hospital are picking up. We have three patients now. Really rough work (smiles).

Did you get a chance to see Leroy & Maxie? Did they say why they hadn't written?

Mama, I wrote a letter to Judge Hill a few days ago. There was a mix-up on my back time—not all of it was given to me as he instructed, so I wrote him asking him to clarify the situation for me. When I told these folks I had written him, they quickly found their error and gave me credit for all my jail time (from Cincy to now). So, would you call Ed and have him have Hill disregard the matter—it has been straightened out & I'm satisfied with the correction.

These folks here will do anything to you that you let them do!

I heard from Kay and Dad the other day—it was good knowing they're OK. Tell Mildred and Cecil [*my aunt and uncle*] I haven't forgotten them, but I'll write soon. Relay my love to them. I'll close for now & write more later. Don't forget the message to Ed for Judge Hill, OK?

Love ya' so,
Ernest

•

Leavenworth Federal Prison, Leavenworth, Kansas
4 October 1972

Mama,

Received your Sunday afternoon letter earlier today. Fred and I are very proud of the developments. I (we) share virtually all of our mail and we have grown closer through the outside happenings. The "domino theory" of interaction is basically true, in regard to the growing interdependence. And, in a real way, there is a dynamic relation between the outside and the inside.

I did write you last week. Hopefully, you've received it by now. If so, let me know in your next letter. I'm well over the flu bug . . . but I have been swamped with my duties around here. It's weird almost, that even here there are not enough hours in the day.

I hope Gwen made it to Louisville. There are some very good people with SCEF. In fact, Walter Collins, my friend who was recently paroled from Texarkana should have been there also. Moreover, I'm communicating with his attorney there—perhaps she met him also. I wrote him only recently requesting information on the bond situation . . . waiting for a reply.

I read of the conference in Cincy, which I presume is the same one Harry attended. If so, I am regretful that he failed to show. One thing in particular I wanted to discuss with him is Faye's situation. Do you remember Don Williams' ex-woman (I guess) from Texarkana? I felt a real solution to her very painful problems could be to go to L.A. and work with Harry. She was enthusiastic about the idea. I regard it as the only immediate hope she has for re-structuring her life into a meaningful and valuable one. She has very serious problems and Texarkana is literally robbing her of her life. Perhaps you could either have Harry communicate to me on this or inform him of it yourself. (Another bomb dropping on you huh? Sorry.) The only snag I see would be housing her and her two kids in a suitable place. She is a good worker, has a dialectical mind, and a good educational background. I'm sure Harry could find immediate employment for her in his area of work. Let me know if this makes sense and/or if you could relay this to Harry. I hesitate to write him so I will, if necessary, at the West 63rd St address if he's still there. Correct me if I'm on the wrong assumption.

The committee of purpose indeed drew up an excellent statement of principles. They are correct and full of healthy life . . . hence, a guide to concrete action. What's Do-Do talking about now? I guess (if history has any value), that conversation over the phone with him was the last one until his next arrest, huh?

I hope the supposition about Ed writing the parole board is a fact!

Wrote Kay a birthday greeting. Almost let the 5th of October catch me without doing so. I teased her about being in the "30s club." Pretty soon, I won't be able to joke with her on that, huh?

Forgive me for the slack of communication on my part. I try not to let too many days pass without writing you. I think of you much more often than that though.

I'll write Fe tonight, too. Got a letter from her today and I'll relay to her all the names of people (outside of the family who wrote letters to my caseworker). Just for the record, OK?

Tonight (I promise myself!) to write Austin (Larry) and Houston prison committee with the hope of putting them in closer contact with y'all. Hopefully, they will contact you soon.

Would you believe I'm developing a stutter in my speech? This I'm trying to overcome . . . it's probably the result of internalizing and repressing too much over the last few years. I'm increasing my public speaking role, perhaps that will have positive effects on my speech as well. But, more than ever, I realize the need to relate more openly and to express my feelings then and there, rather than harbor them for great lengths of time.

I'll close for now. Still haven't written Dad—heard from him lately? Love to our friends. Take care of yourself.

With love,
Ernest

1973

TEXAS DEPARTMENT OF CORRECTIONS

Unit Diagnostics

Date   15 February 1973

Inmate's No.   230064

Name Marion Ernest McMillan

To: Mrs. Eva C. McMillan   Relation: Mother

RFD, Street or Box No.: 2623 East Illinois Ave

- #131   City Dallas   State   Texas

TO THE PERSON RECEIVING THIS LETTER – (IMPORTANT, READ THIS)

All inmate's mail is opened, censored, and recorded by OFFICIALS. Inmates may receive not more than three letters a week from any one person on their correspondence and visiting lists. These letters must be limited to two pages. You may use one sheet and write on the front and back if you wish. Please address the inmate by name and number. If these rules are not observed the letter will be returned to the sender.

Any money to be deposited to the account of an inmate must be in the form of a postal money order or cashier's check made payable to the INMATE TRUST FUND. They must be mailed to P.O. Box 60, Huntsville, Texas 77340. The correct name and number of the inmate to receive the money must be included or the funds will be returned to the sender. Please include a return address on all envelopes directed to the Inmate Trust Fund.

You can see by all the official rhetoric on this "stationary" that I've made it on down to TDC! I'm OK. I left Wed. morning and we arrived here the same afternoon. I'm glad that I got a chance to write you before leaving DCT. You should have received it the same day I left. There was no way I could have called before leaving though I knew a bus was leaving as early as Tuesday, I didn't know for sure if I would be with it until I was told so Wed morning.

Wade Cooper James has some property of mine to be released to you. Everything was so hectic that I couldn't make better arrangements. You should have received a phone call from him, and I'm trusting that, by now, all the rest of my property is in your hands. In the vanilla envelope is the statement I've been working on; it begins, "Freedom loving people of Dallas . . ."and is four and a half pages long. I hope you have it. Please let me know. I am told that I will be here for a month to a month and a half.

While I'm here, I won't be able to have visitors. But, when I'm finally classified and sent to wherever they decide to send me, I'll write and let you know so you can visit. I will be in need of some money very shortly. Enclosed, find a slip that has to be filled out and returned along with the money order. It's to be sent to a different post office box than the one I receive letters, so be sure you get that clear. The procedures are different than Leavenworth. I'll write later about the visiting procedures, they're different, too.

The visible tactics and attitudes toward the men are different also—"discipline" a la mode de Texas, but I know what their objectives are, so it doesn't bother me so much. Maxie is here too, but I only see him at chow. When I get to an assigned place, it will be a little better. (About the same sort of change in the army—from boot camp to regular service).

There are a lot of familiar faces from school days, you know. The kind who you always wonder, "what happened to . . ." Well, if they ain't dead, then they're in the Army or prison I believe. I can receive pictures here, so don't hesitate to send me some from time to time. I will be seeking to find out the procedures of the parole board and my status in relation to it. I'll let you know when I find out. Let me hear how things are going in Dallas. Give everyone my best regards. I'll write again tomorrow. Take care.

Love ya,
Ernest

•

Diagnostic Unit, Texas Department of Corrections
17 February 1973
To   Mrs. Eva C. McMillan

Greetings! I hope everyone is fine and in good spirits. Trust you received my last letter (written 2-15-73). How is everything? Things here are about as expected; except these guys all take their Hoot Gibson John Wayne roles seriously. I believe some of these folks would just shrivel up and die if there wasn't a war to fight, or a poor person to bust. They can't even imagine the roles reversed (and that is a plus for our corner). Some of the brothers mutter, "They treat us far better than I'd treat them," but then their own eyes betray their words and I know better. If hate and anger were the sole forces necessary to bring about a change, perhaps what they say would be true. But, since emotions (whatever they be) are not capable of producing desired results, then what these brothers feel in terms of pain, suffering and isolation is only the crude beginnings of real awareness. We have a long way to go.

I don't have too much to say. I'm writing primarily because I said I would be writing the next day, in my last letter. Seeing what the situation is, I will do exactly what I said. I don't want to create any unnecessary alarms. Communication will be important. If you fail to hear from me at some point, then you'll know something is very wrong. So, I'm planning to write you at least a "hello" once very week. OK?

What's going on in Zim's [*Judge James Zimmermann, who sentenced me to ten years*] court? If it's still just sitting, there, I urge you to please contact Janet or the Black lawyer in Houston to see if they would draw up a writ of habeas corpus for the federal court—based upon Perini's and

Zim's indifference/laziness whatever to move the writ. You should first have Perini [*Vincent Perini, who along with Frank Hernandez represented me on the state charges, later referred to occasionally as "V"*] give you a photocopy of the writ and the evidence. Tell him it's for the record or anything. Then, Janet [*Stockard, a deeply committed and trusted attorney in Austin, Texas*] and or someone could just put it into another form for the federal courts; get it notarized and boom we're on our way. Please let me know if you have any problems in doing this, OK?

Give my love and regards to all. Did you get the statement from the brothers at DCJ?

Hope to hear from you soon.

Love ya,
Ernest
(Hope you can understand my printing!)

•

Diagnostic Unit, Texas Department of Corrections
6 March 1973
To   Mrs. Eva C. McMillan

Received your letters (three!) dated 2-28, 3-1, and 3-4—got all of them today. Also, I have a letter from Jackie today. You know it's good to hear from home! The news from here is that I'll be classified soon, probably before the week is out and possibly as early as tomorrow! If that happens, I will be able to receive visitors this coming weekend. As soon as I am classified, I'll send you the info as to the location of the "farm" I'm to be on. I'll enclose directions, too.

It's a shame that only two adults will be allowed to visit—so we'll have to arrange things to suit their rules. I learned also today, officially, that parole is not a legal right but an extended "grace" from the lords of state. How brutally arrogant are these yokels. The shameful thing is that it is only a true reflection of the total absence of people's power in this state. As long as things exist in this status quo, anything we gain is truly a wretched grace.

I am burning with something I can only call rage. My release date, according to their calendars, is 1981, and (if I'm a "good boy") the date is '78. Due to the machination of the parole system, I do not expect or strive for a parole release. They have a diabolic plan: a convict must work his way out of prison i.e. crawl, crawl, crawl. In the feds, they at least looked to the outside in considering parole . . . but here it is nothing of the sort—a person can't even become eligible for parole unless he has the approval (grace) of the TDC administration. I'm sorry to have to relate this ugly fact but it is, and therefore we must deal with it. So much for that.

I have luxuriously fed on the news of the court hearing, Walter Collins' message, Sandra's call, Ohene at the zoo, Oretha's dream, Osorio, Ranger, Fred's case, your health, Jackie's being, the Sudan, and Wounded Knee's challenge. I don't want to sound as though none of it registered—it all did singularly and in total! Comment when I see you.

I don't like what seems to be happening to the statement I wrote. Although I'm afraid of it in some ways, it's important that it (1) get to the people personally and (2) that I know honestly the effect, reception, and comments from the people. I don't think anyone understands—and now I'm sure it's in the wrong hands—tied! Please tell Jackie I'll write tomorrow. The guards refuse to bring the pencil sharpener and my pencil has just about had it.

I received the $10 money order, and also got another $10 money order the following day. Who dat? (Hope your eyes are handling this scribbling OK.)

Yes, try for the grant it sounds out-a-sight. I've been wondering a while ago as to just what foundations to try—to no avail. Mary Greene with *Sesame Street* would prove valuable help in that area also. Dean

Kelly. It's not as far-fetched an idea as it may seem now. Many credible and effective community organizations are actually sought out by some foundations. If the guy from Boulder, Colorado fails to come through, get ideas from Kelly or Greene OK?

I'll write Jackie tomorrow—give her my all. I plan to write Charlie, too—he's also on my waiting list.

My fingers (et. al) are crossed for Janet! I hope the latest method works.

No trouble around here yet—I'm living in the cut, refused to be provoked, cajoled fo' time. The time is not too far though when every resource I'm able to call on will be needed . . . spiritual included.

Tell Bettie and Angie I'll be in contact soon.

Hope someone can get to the hearing if there's to be one. It seems that just a statement from Zims (written) is the only formality—but in case this is not so and there will be a hearing, please see if someone with a legal inkling can be there.

Cancel on the wedding plans for Maxie & Vickie—another point for the state! I'm sorry Brewer went through so much trouble to no avail. I would enjoy seeing him but my real spiritual advisor is in KC—Fuzz! He's too much.

Hope the phone call from San didn't startle you! Once, I gave you her address to send posters and buttons, too, but we were all so busy . . . Anyway, she's great—saved my life—Kay's met her.

Mama, I hated the thought that sometimes I take you, Jack, Kat, etc. for granted. Now, I realize that's what love is all about— knowing and giving—accepting. We are living Rocks.

Kiss Ohene for me, love to Oretha, Fe et al.

Hope to see you soon.
Ernest

●

Walls Unit, Texas Department of Corrections
29 March 1973
To   Mrs. Eva C. McMillan

I don't know what's with the mail situation around here! I've only writ-ten you a couple of letters in the past ten days, but you should have long received them. I'm pleased you took the action you did. You know I'm not going to cry wolf—ever. Perhaps, after playing back the recording from our visit, they decided that they would find out if we really would implement action on non-communication between us (smiles?). Besides the long-distance charges, your call will have other effects (on the posi-tive side) down the way . . . if nothing but a slight hesitation from their schemes.

Glad to know you were in touch with Harry. I will correspond with him at that address if he likes just as soon as possible. That means ninety days or less, if the rule changes through the courts regarding our ancient mail "privileges." Oh, yes and that address for Angie is the one I had also—thank goodness—I wrote her a few days ago but I guess she wasn't in receipt of it when she wrote you. Did you ever discover her date of birth? I still feel pretty sure it's the 30th of April, but you know how I am with recalling dates.

I'm working the three to eleven shift at the hospital now, regularly. That's the main reason why I haven't been writing, as I should. I do man-age to maintain at least one or two a week though. Usually, at those hours that I'm not working, I would devote to reading and writing but now those hours are busy, busy ones. It's hard getting adjusted to the new schedule and if I don't see a way I'll try to get my hours changed to another shift. The hours I now have kill all the time I have usually spent studying law/library etc. As it is now, I only have a couple of hours for that.

I certainly hope you track down the source and the contents of that leaflet. Yes, I believe this could be just the thang, too. In my property from DCJ are 3 letters from C.G. [*Curtis Gaines, the alleged police agent who became a leader in the initial Black Panther Party until his expulsion upon discovery of his alleged paid cooperation with the police*]. You should check them out to perceive the real style of his rantings and ravings. There are three letters but I think one of the envelopes was torn so I put one letter along with another. Also, in case you want to really pursue this thing: there's a brother in DCJ named John Dupree. I wrote him several letters concerning my position on Gaines/Vanguard. He would relay them to you if you desired them. Perhaps CG got wind of the article in *Voice* (the joint statement) or maybe my conversation with Do Do let him know just what my real position is. Whatever his motivation, it's based on fear and I'm certain that Fred/Charlie et. al., involved must be prepared to meet extreme actions from this sort of person. Dangerous is the word. He can't last, but being the snake he is you ought to be prepared for the worst kind of schemes. For one, the junkie mentality (many of those he has influence over) would do anything for a fix, so he has a "killer" squad. On the quiet side, you should keep Buffalo abreast of these developments, OK.

Who is coming to visit Sunday? I hope Ohene is planning to come, also if Charlie is coming, I hope there'll be a clearer picture of the happenings in Dallas.

If there's no action on the writ from Zim's meeting by the end of this week, would you see if Janet or someone could file a writ of mandamus on my behalf? It's a request to Austin to order Zim to obey his duty. I have one prepared but thought maybe Janet could do it faster if she agreed. It is necessary at this time.

Is the film "Four Walls" the one with Dallas SNCC or what? Yes, I know Stanley Wise. I don't think he'll be of any help really. From experience, I know he's not very reliable, but it's no harm in you gaining some of that experience too (smile). I wish Harry luck.

Do you have our Black legislators' addresses? Please send them to me. How is Jackie? She hasn't answered my letters. I received $3 from someone. I don't know who. The date was the 26th though. If it was Kay, give her my best wishes and love. As far as the money situation goes, I'm alright until the last week in April or so. Dad sent $20 a week ago. Good shape for a month or so.

Also, I got the "Dear Ernie" from Fe! She's in a helluva fantasy world in the last analysis. I hope our ruptured relationship doesn't damage y'alls. (It shouldn't be that way.) I'm awaiting the papers from Ed. All this paperwork is de facto. It has no meaning. I've felt single for a long time (smiles & serious). Take care. I'll write more later. My writing is terrible!

Love ya,
Ernest

•

Walls Unit, Texas Department of Corrections
3 April 1973
To   Mrs. Eva C. McMillan

Yesterday, I sat down to write you—I got a couple of notes off to Dad & Kat and was late to work. I hope this letter finds you as well and strong in spirit as always.

It was good visiting with you, Kat & Ohene Sunday. I hope you made it back to Dallas safely. It was really kind of that lady to take you and Mrs. Johnson back—save so much time and trouble.

When you write Karen and Harry, please tell them that they will be on my visiting list in a month or so and that I'll be writing as soon as I can. If that address for Harry (and Kay, too) changes, please let me know as soon as you can.

I'm going to subscribe (or try to) a few papers that send free subscriptions to prisoners. I know you haven't had much of a chance, but would you see about those books from international publishers as soon as you can.

I think Ohene is really growing into some fine character. I think his overzealousness into mischievous things is pretty natural and possibly could be the framework that adult-like assertiveness will stem from. I'm anxious to hook up with him. I hope there won't be any hassles with Fe because I'm thinking of some prolonged type get togethers (trips together, etc.). We'll see, (again).

I plan to write Charlie tonight (hopefully). He has become somewhat slow since Fred's departure from Siberia.

Please let me know more about that leaflet as soon as you can. I have a feeling that you still haven't received all my letters. The ones you mentioned receiving were late enough, so perhaps the one where I had the instructions (request) to Jan is still on its way, too.

I must go for now—I'll write some more tomorrow—a promise. Take care.

Love ya,
Ernest

•

Walls Unit, Texas Department of Corrections
6 April 1973
To   Mrs. Eva C. McMillan

I hope this letter finds you well. I am up early this morning and it seems like the best and perhaps the only schedule I can maintain to get things done. It feels good to rise with the sun. It was taking quite a bit of adjusting (you might say) to get my writings and studying done while working at night which have been my prime time for such. So now, getting up at five and doing these things allows me ample time. I'm working from three to eleven at night and I guess I've gotten into the swing of it. (Now, there's no doubt that my shift will be changed again (smiles).

I received the newspaper last night—it was very interesting! I really liked your article. Now I know I'm going to have to watch what I say to you (just kidding).

Also heard from Angela! It was such a lovely letter—just a powerful letter in its natural simplicity. She wrote on the very kind of paper I used to draw horses on, etc. and tried to spell "vary much" on.

Heard Angela D. on the radio—day before yesterday! It was quite a shock to hear her making a speech over the censored prison radio. Quite a pleasant one though. Every now and then, we slip one in (ha!). She was speaking from Houston and it was the very first time that I've ever heard her voice. She expressed herself very clearly, although it seemed to be quite a struggle to do so. I guess it's her desire to be completely honest yet plain as possible in such complex matters. One question asked her (probably someone seeking to embarrass her) was on the incident of Russia "invading" Czechoslovakia. She went into a thing very carefully and yet explicit . . . in less than four minutes she had presented a very complete picture. Something like that would have taken me hours if ever to explain. She is very brilliant. She predicted by her own analysis, socialist USA by the (or before the year) 2000. To which she received a thunderous applause.

Any word from Janet on my request about the writ of mandamus?

Everyone here is awaiting the court's ruling on open correspondence for the prisoners. It was originally granted, just recently, but the system or Dallas County asked for a stay of execution. My understanding is that the deadline was yesterday. So, we're looking for something soon. It would be indispensable to win that constitutional right back! Well, I'll close for now.

Please tell all I say hello and that the keeper of the castle is under an unliftable seize!

Have you heard from that "lawyer's" folks yet? I understand he wrote them to contact you soon. I hope something will be done for him before the month is out. Keep me in touch . . . I ain't heard from you, in a letter all week! Love ya' though. Kiss Jackie, Yiki, 'Hene for me.

Unity! Unity! Unity!
Ernest

•

Walls Unit, Texas Department of Corrections
21 April 1973
To   Mrs. Eva C. McMillan

Dear Mama, I finally found the address of the publishing company and I have already written them. If I have any trouble receiving those books, I'll let you know because I will exhaust every legal means to maintain the right to read and study.

I also wrote V and I was forewarned about his possible reaction to my letter by your report of the conversation with him. I wrote a two-sentence letter asking him to send me the date of the writ and asked were there any changes in the status of the writ. It really appears as though his interests are super-independent of our needs. I won't be able to tolerate him not responding to my requests. If he does, it may be grounds enough (along with Zim's action—rather, inaction) to go directly into the federal courts. I received the official notification that my parole eligibility is June 1974. You know I'm not sitting around waiting on that regardless of V & Z's intentions.

The meeting in Atlanta was a gas! I hadn't realized it was such a well-attended conference. Do you have any copies of some of the speeches?

Glad to know you heard from Harriette (Harriette Morgan, my first true love! We were a serious, passionate pair whose mother detested our relationship mainly because I was from the "wrong side of the tracks"; forbidding us to marry). Perhaps, we will be able to write and visit in a few ... that is if I stretch the list some. Is her last name still Knox or did she say? I'll try a business letter to the folks in D.C. later this week.

Is there a halfway house for prisoners in Dallas? There is such a terrific need for one. Many have asked for assistance and it's gotten out of the personal individual thing. I wish UDPP could help at least ten or twelve men find jobs/places to stay for the remainder of the year. We could really have something going for us when people see we are serious and filling some real needs. I view this sort of project as a priority and I want to talk to someone about it soon. There's one in Houston but it's of no help for men from D. What is needed is a large house—the men here could help pay rent—assistance in finding jobs, educational programs, etc. and we could provide a real service. Check into how the one in Houston was founded. It's easy. Churches/clubs etc. could give support.

I hope to see y'all Sunday. I don't believe I can retain my thoughts another week or even last that long, so get up here when you can (smiles).

Watergate is a good example in the process of revealing who (and what form) the real crooks are. Law and order rhetoric seems to have its real purpose and intent revealed when such devious acts occur.

You know what all of us TDC prisoners have in common? We have committed an act against the state of Texas or rather we've been forced to take a position of opposition against the state machinery. Some starting point, huh? I'll write more later.

•

Walls Unit, Texas Department of Corrections
28 April 1973
To   Mrs. Eva C. McMillan

I started writing you earlier today in response to the beautiful letter I received from you yesterday, but so much has happened since this morning that I had to scrap that letter and start writing anew. It is now 5:30 PM Sunday evening.

Charlie, Jackie, and Yiki visited today, and it was a great visit with much meaningful and needed dialogue. We covered practically all the ground needed and just in time, too, because it seems as though the machinery here has been provoked into initiating a direct attack against me with very thin and transparent motives.

I am now in solitary awaiting the administrators "court" to decide fit punishment for a most fabricated charge of "insubordination." Although they call this part of prison lock-up and I still have all my property (and writing privileges) in my possession, it is still solitary confinement. In fact, for them to place me officially in "the hole," all they require is to remove my property (papers, cigarettes, pens, etc.) and close a second door. Anyway, this is a pre-trial status and I'm told that "court" will not be until next week.

Shortly after chow, I was approached by a senile lieutenant, who told me he wanted my hair cut. (It was a clear attempt at provocation to me right then.) So, I paused and took a couple of deep breaths. He then said after a lengthy silence, "Are you going to cut your hair?" I said I'll think about it . . . figuring that that was it and it's over, you know. (Even if I wanted to, I could not magically produce some clippers right then and there as his attitude strongly suggested.) So, his response to my calm dry answer was like—boom! I was handed over to a higher officer and immediately told that I was to be locked up for refusing to obey an order. If this wasn't real, it would be funny but it's real . . . unleashed harassment that must have been seething for a while and reached its climax with revenge because of the things we've been legally pursuing on behalf of the prison population. I think Jackie and Charlie's visit had something to do with it, as we had very nosey neighbors during their visit.

I hope to see Ed or John soon! I'm anxious to have a court of Law review this matter. I will not back up one inch now that everything's out in the open—all the formalities are tossed aside. There are many other things that must be done. I think you know what they are. What can Jan do!

Maybe you or someone can arrange a special visit as it's allowed for many families who live as far away as Dallas and cannot make it on the weekend because of their workdays in conflict with present visiting days.

Let me hear from you soon. Tell Ragsdale [*Paul, State Representative*], as my letter to him also may very easily be another reason for my status now. Print the letter if you wish and if he agrees. Also, the guy in Washington—N.P.P.—may have some colleagues in this area who can drop in.

Let me hear from you soon. I will be writing every day to you. I am afraid that my letter supply—stamps—is very low. I completely forgot to ask Jackie if she could leave me some bread. So, send me a few dollars as soon as you can. I just signed up for ten dollars, but it will probably bounce if something is not sent very soon. That may be another case (smiles).

I'm fine so far. There has been no physical violence and I don't expect any at this point. I am refusing to eat all meals served to me in their special individual style. So, that means I'll be fasting until I'm released from solitary. Let's see just what kind of support we have around this state OK?

I do have time for a lot of writing finally, but the irony is I'm short of paper. Ain't that a gas?

Take care. Don't worry, just remember the fact that for every action, there is a reaction, and I can handle anything they throw without a doubt because I know that struggle is the only way.

Maybe Ragsdale or Johnson can call these folks. Perhaps, this is the way we can help present the Pardon issue to them finally, huh? Other than the fact that I'm no longer able to develop the projects we've started here (for the time being), which hurts because so much is needed and we were beginning to move toward it, I'm in high morale and strongest spirit.

Prepare for the worst to achieve the Best!
Ernest

•

Retrieve Unit, Texas Department of Corrections
5 May 1973
To   Mrs. Eva C. McMillan

Dear Mother,

Just received two more letters from the walls bringing the total up to 5 from there. Does that sound about right? Also, received two today you wrote right before the rally and right afterward. Got a letter from Fuzz forwarded from the walls. He sent Fe & Ohene's flick along (that I had given him for the campaign while in Kansas). He said he would have liked to have kept them (???). If you have some around the house, could you send him some? These I can't spare (smiles).

It was so good hearing from you! It was like being apart from you those hectic days while I was in the hole, all the way through to now. I felt almost emotionally drained when I completed them. It's not anything "wrong," sort of like reading a powerful novel that relates so closely to one's own experience. Dig? Now is the time for me to ask you—ain't it about time for you to write something for publishing? Really! Mama you are sooo beautiful. It's inexpressible for me to relate how I feel in reflection on your letters and you going to DCJ before going home from work and writing letters and catching up on UDPP, before even tackling household chores. I do wish you had the security, etc. to devote as much time as you saw fit to movement/people matters. That day will come but I think you know how I feel about that.

Also, got a letter from Dad written to the Walls May 16th. He said he'd heard from you, plus a card from my keepers at the walls. He expressed concern and solidarity. He also said he'd sent $10. I'll write him tonight. I wrote Eddie Bernice tonight—possibly she'll be contact-ing you soon, as I enclosed your address and phone number. Also, got the letter off to the State Supreme Court—phew!—glad to be through with that. Surprised to hear that Vee had written Zim! Please tell me what he said when we visit . . . I brought enough stamps and envelopes where I'll have no further excuse to not write you any less than twice a week, OK! Yeah, you had guessed my situation but everything's straight now. I've got things budgeted to where I'll be able to make it on existing funds until July or so. Perhaps, by then, my situation will have altered to a more favorable one, huh?

Yes, I'm into the swing of things, labor-wise and health wise. When there's little choice in the matter, my ole body somehow provides what's required of it. Sometimes, I'm often amazed at what seemingly is impos-sible physically is really not such a difficulty. Just as in the struggle: by doing, we gain experience, expertise and knowledge and actually rise to greater levels. Being a mule however is just too much of a demand, espe-cially when there are zero benefits for self and the collective! Therefore, this manner of living (?) is out of touch with today. Nature herself thus enters upon the scene to see what the hell's wrong and effects a cure as always. It's nothing at all mysterious to me and I'm trying to find ways to aid nature's process.

Have Denise send books from Timbuktu to Book Store please, via certified mail. I have a better chance of receiving them thusly. I hadn't heard from her in so long I thought she'd quit relating to us Texans. Please ask her if she'd received my letter from Leavenworth (Jan '73). Darn! Almost out of space.

Well, I'll see you Sunday. I'll have myself together by then and hope-fully we'll get to cover plenty of ground. I do want to hear your speech, so don't forget. It felt good to know I was thought of at the rally. Wow! And Clay Smothers is only making tactful adjustments if you ask me—it must be pretty lonely out on that reactionary limb, especially when peo-ple are so hip to him and laugh in his face. He can't return to the masses because he makes a few diplomatic responses. And probably never. Easy mau-mau.

Victory through unity!

P.S. Still no letter from Ed yet.

•

Retrieve Unit, Texas Department of Corrections
27 May 1973
To   Mrs. Eva C. McMillan

Dear Mama,

It was great seeing you guys! I guess in all the excitement, I forgot to mention several things. One is that I start college tomorrow (I mentioned it to Charlie so perhaps he's relayed it to you). I'm taking a history course (world history from the Western capitalistic view of course!) and Business (which is even more pitiful—the American way, private enterprise, individualism, etc. et. al!). I think I'll find some interesting aspects, especially if we have a chance to free expression. I think I'll graduate from junior college with these two subject hours. I think that's all the hours I'll need for an AA degree (Associate of Arts) but I'll check to make sure.

The other thing was to see if Ed will be coming down here soon. I need to know for sure, so I can't go for "I'll tries" or "maybes" etc. If he says he can't come, see if Jim or John can come, please. I need to discuss those legal matters we rapped about.

I'll write Harry, Harriette, and San tonight or tomorrow and I'll also try to get to the bottom as to why Charlie has been arbitrarily removed from my list. I'll try to write him tonight also but the letter may not get out until the issue is resolved.

Kat and Jackie (Yiki and Ohene) were just beautiful, too. We got cut really short on the time-side. I wasn't really conscious that so little time was left. If I had been aware, we could have gotten them in sooner. (I just looked back over my writing! The slant change corresponds to my changing positions, I'm writing (awkwardly) in bed!

Mama, I've received many reports and comments about seeing you on TV. I'm really sorry I missed it. You have won much respect from many quarters, you know. I think you ought to save all the speeches you make. We'll get that book together one way or another, huh? Well, I'll close for now so I can get the other letters off before lights are turned off.

I couldn't resist calling Ohene when I was returning to the yard and almost got another case (smiles). Do I love that man-child! We had a little session while you and Charlie were trying to straighten out the mail list "oversight"—he is "a helluva boy" as the Liberians say.

Got to go. Just wanted to drop a note of greetings. Relay my solidarity to Fred. If it's not too embarrassing to him, please tell him I'm glad he understands my primary motive and concern in the letter to Charlie? Ask him to drop me a line please.

Take care.

Unity for Struggle, Struggle for Unity,
Ernest

•

Retrieve Unit, Texas Department of Corrections
22 June 1973
To   Mrs. Eva C. McMillan

Greetings Mama,

By the time you receive this letter, we will have cleared up a lot of things so I'm writing now to discuss something I'm sure we won't get off into Sunday—time allowed to visit being what it is! In a way that ain't too cool because very seldom do we ever rap about feelings, fears . . .

personal matters. We have such an ordered business approach (would you believe?) and I realize it's such a necessity given the overall problems that confront us as well as the short and rigid atmosphere in which we converse. (We manage to get done what has to be done, and that in itself calls for a helluva unity!) So, I'm not complaining, just anxious for the day when we can relate unconscious of time and place—in peace.

Well, again I salute you! Embrace you with love . . . for you've done it again. You have again revealed to me your <u>courage</u> and <u>faith</u>. Yes. I'm referring to the news of Fe's new entanglement. (I mean marriage.) I say "courage" because I know it took an awful struggle with self, words, emotions, and conviction, to so resolutely share the "news." And, I say "faith" because you believed so thoroughly in your power to express the truth, the need for it and finally the faith in me to deal with it. I guess these two qualities are so interdependent . . . without courage there cannot be any faith and <u>vice versa</u>.

So now, I must try to muster some of those same energies. First of all, I want to say we don't deal with Fe's marriage by saying there are so many other women in the world for me. That to me ain't dealing with it, rather copping out to some evasion of the real subject. To me, the thing for me to try to handle is, how do I feel having someone I once loved dearly choose to share her life with another man? I won't go off into <u>her</u> reasons, motivations, and feelings (as I see it).

Maybe, you'll realize hers when I try to explain myself. I <u>have</u> gone off deeply into her side but these two pages won't allow me to express both. So, this letter is intentionally one-sided on the surface, but solely for economy of space. OK?

There is a source within me that I'd like very much to wiggle my feeling so that things will <u>sound</u> correct. I'm struggling very hard with that desire to play games with my feelings for the sake of being proper and thus more acceptable. But I don't want that kind of thing.

There was never a time in my life that I ever actively sought and tried to win a woman that I really wanted. I mean that every woman that

I've ever gone with was the aggressor (and I the aggressee?). Yes. This includes Pat, Harriette, et. al—Fe. I guess a psychiatrist would say that this was due to a fear of being rejected. A thing I accused Fe of in my last letter, remember? I did exercise a degree of control over selection—though it was minimal—to encourage those that were reasonably OK and discourage those who were repulsive. As you can see though, very little assertiveness (aggressiveness) was on my part, a sort of passive acceptance or rejection of her advances.

Where Fe comes in is that I just sort of learned to like her—to love her. (I felt gratitude for her sacrifices and a sense of obligation to her.) Rather than look for qualities, I looked for safety. Once these criteria were filled, I then looked for things in her that I could call good. So really, my real feeling toward her was indifference, even though at the time I would con myself into believing I "cared." Dig, only when she got hip and began to reject me (through subtle signs or loud declarations), did I begin to try to save something, to make something real or in other words to win her love. But, with earlier "loves," I'd usually turn just as cold or split altogether.

Now, perhaps Fe utilized the divorce and remarriage as a gimmick to influence my passion (which was really only ego) for her. I'd like to believe that (smiles) but I don't believe that's true. Even if it were, it wouldn't work, for I have changed.

Now, I demand that my woman be stable, sharp, expressive, principled, etc. rather than just dig me. I can't even picture myself with a weak, dependent, "moon-eye" type anymore. And, the opposite used to be true with me. I used to strongly resent intelligent, independent types because they bore a sure threat to my almighty ego. Fe's action helped to awaken me to my real motivation toward her. So, in a lot of ways, I am freed of the miserable communion—that is marriage behind bars.

•

Retrieve Unit, Texas Department of Corrections
25 June 1973
8:00 AM
To   Mrs. Eva C. McMillan

Dear Mother,

Seeing you, Jack, Kat, David, and Yiki was really wonderful. The presence of your strength and unity is the source of mine.

I was "commanded" by the brother to relay his deep appreciation to you and all for bringing Francis down with you. He had been very distressed all week in not hearing from her.

Oh yes, and I found out later that a great number of the men from my wing had been tripping on David, Kat and Yiki. It seems that they went for a stroll to the "pond" while we were visiting—I guess everyone was identifying with the peace, love, and freedom they so naturally reflected. I was told by several, every little thing they did—Yiki almost fell in the water, too! The brothers thought it very cool and I can dig it because the only time we can view a tender moment, it is usually artificial and interrupted by the words "brought to you by Coca Cola, Salem, or etc. . . ."

8:45 PM
What a day. This morning when I got the letter it seemed as though it was too wet to work but we were all called to work about 8:30. Foiled again! Anyway, since then, I received your letter written on Sat (also one from Kay!).

I haven't written Eddie B, Janet, or Charlie yet, but I will soon. At present, I'm trying to prepare for a test (history) and John's expected visit. I guess I'll burn a lot of midnight oil tonight.

I hope you remember to contact Eddie B. so that John will have all the info necessary for his visit. For example, you know when writing me to include my number. It is the same with visiting, especially if someone wanted to make an easy excuse for not letting you see me. So, therefore, it's important to have my name and my prison number as well. I think pretty soon and at the rate we're going, the entire population will have a number rather than a name for identification. In some area prisons, it's already true. "Big Brother" is watching you and me.

Haven't received the papers today. If I haven't by tomorrow, I'll have another issue to impress upon attorneys.

Oh yes, if Ed wants any info from me in establishing the fact of "exhaustion of state remedies," have him to let me know. It's really disturbing to know he has not received one letter from me since my confinement in TDC—cold-blooded!

Do you have any info regarding the date and itinerary of Bernice's tour? I hope it is soon. (I would advise her that she shouldn't let her guests know of her plans —a real surprise visit.)

How did the showing of the film go? Have you made the interview— my son's recognized guardian (smiles)? One more question—request, rather. If you hear from Harriette and if she's having a kickback on mail like before, it may be due to her lack of writing two pages or less.

I haven't heard from her in a week or so and I had a note from the mailroom officer about her letters being too lengthy. Anyway, she may have tried to write me and failed to reach me for that reason. Then again, she may not have written at all (who knows?). Don't call her—if I don't hear from her by Wed or so I'll write her again. Please send those photos from my luggage. I was under the impression that you said they were not to be found.

Things are as tight as before. Desperation is the word for today. There will be no peace until some justice reigns. We know it, they know it, so the need to carry through to the end are our most legitimate objectives. We'll never turn back. I am in good spirits and health. Without the enlightened masses, we would be nothing—perhaps the same status as goldfish in a small bowl—certainly nothing more than it. From the prison to the community—solidarity! From the community to the prison—solidarity!

Revolutionary Justice!
E.M.

P.S. Did you locate the names/addresses of the state directors? If not, I'll get them & send it to you. OK?

•

Retrieve Unit, Texas Department of Corrections
1 July 1973
Sun., 10:00 PM
To   Mrs. Eva C. McMillan

Dearest Mother,

It was good to hear from you again. I got your 6-28 letter yesterday. I'll admit that I was disappointed to learn you have yet to receive the two letters I wrote this week! If you'll notice from the content of my letters over the last two weeks, I have been deliberately restrained (well, anyway you'll notice it from the <u>fraction</u> of letters actually received). But, knowing the anguish and worry you must be undergoing due to the systematic delay (or destruction) of my correspondence to you, I have been forced to take some corrective steps. The proper authorities have been notified of these encroachments, so relief is soon on the way.

I want you to know that I am well as can be expected under the "normal" circumstances of daily confinement in a Texas prison. There have been no further attacks, other than what one normally faces daily as a typical convict on a prison farm unit. I'm in the population and undergoing the basic routine that everyone else in white experiences. OK? Don't worry. My major concern at present is knowing that you aren't falsely alarmed as to my well-being. When desperation and terror are the chief forms of reaction, state lackeys usually strive to intimidate an object with the potential of shedding light to the real basis of its fears. The intimidation is intended as a two-edged sword; and in this case, you, as well as myself.

You see, to my keepers, a letter from a prisoner has absolutely no value, not even the eight cents that looms on the right-hand corner—since they didn't buy it, nor can use it. To a prisoner, a letter possesses infinite or incalculable value. This, they are well aware. Secondly, the only entity maintaining a degree of sacredness to them is their own hides. And, in the course of these most dynamic days (in the surge of the oppressed to be free of oppression in all forms), you can probably imagine how reckless the oppressor can be in protection of the hide! Witness the Pentagon papers, the Watergate scandal, Vietnam, etc., etc., etc., etc. And as Dylan sang, "You don't have to be a weatherman to see which way the wind is blowing."

I really feel that if we were of any other relation—besides mother-son—a serious attempt would be made to remove you from my mailing list altogether. If fascism were "firm and secure," even this wouldn't be given a second thought. But, for now they're doing in actuality—the same thing in a shilly shallying way. You see, every day you are being recognized more and more as a true champion of the people's struggle . . . and to the anti-people forces, the obscene that adds to agitation, and a bunch of other blankety-blanks. But, since it naturally follows that the true enemies of the Enemy are my comrades, brothers, and sisters, I have no problem with that. I believe you're aware of this previously submerged attitude toward you, but it is quite possible that the next time I visit with you, you will behold a new gallery of faces and we'll both have to go through the trouble of learning an entirely new slate of names!

All sides are preparing for the trip of our Austin friends, so I do hope they will not exhibit naiveté and be led around. From every indication, this will not be so and I want to make sure that they are the asserters rather than the assertees. Dig?

I did not forget that Fe has been victimized by the system. I was though and perhaps (unwisely) dealing (trying to deal, rather) with one specific aspect of the problem.

Congrats on the office! And no, I have not seen F. Cruz! (?) Haven't rec'd *Voice, Patriot, African World,* books from Denise, or photos from you yet? Have there been any attempts to mail any of these things to me?

Close for now, maw-maw. I'll write again tomorrow. The more I write, the more "evidence" I accumulate . . . Take care and hope to see someone soon.

Love ya,
Ernest

•

Retrieve Unit, Texas Department of Corrections
2 July 1973
3:00 PM
To   Mrs. Eva C. McMillan

Hello Mother,

Trust by now you've received my last letter written 7-2-73. In it, I related about the beautiful visit from the "southerners" and my notification from the Supreme Court of Texas that Zimmermann had finally acted on my writ by denying it. I hope this letter finds you well and in the best frame of mind. How's Jackie doing? Please give her my love (a la special!) and best wishes. I will get on the ball today and write Kay, Jan and Charlie. I went to the store and stocked up on stamps and writing material so I ain't got no 'scuses now! (smiles) It's kinda funny but the local store doesn't have legal pads for sale anymore. Wonder why? I hope you'll excuse this notebook paper. This is the best I could do . . . not very much room to get down with.

We're off today for some reason. Someone says this day is a holiday to celebrate someone's independence and freedom from tyranny, injustice, and inequality. The only freedom that exists in this nation is the freedom of capitalists and their flunkies to invade nations, communities, and households, the liberty to suck the blood, muscle and energies of workers for the profit of insatiable parasites, and the kind of equality that allows one-sixth of the world's population to control 25 percent of <u>all</u> the wealth. From these actual conditions, it isn't hard to see who's actually celebrating and who's seriously meditating on the end of bourgeois freedom. Long life to the righteous struggle of revolutionary workers and all oppressed peoples! Long life to all peoples who can find no harmony with <u>any</u> form of exploitation!

I was moved to know Kwesi had made such a decision on his own to re-join the struggle in Dallas. I have no way of pinpointing it at present but I feel he's arrived at a mature stage of viewing himself and submerging himself to real commitments. He's come such a long way given the fact that it had been so obviously expected (via his environment) that his life was to be that of a vagabond, or the likes. I know you will, but I'd like to emphasize his real need for encouragement. Sometimes, it used to make me so sick that his emotional requirements were of the level of a child. I mean simply the same means you would visualize having Ohene or Yiki do something—coaxing, flattering, etc. I guess we all have such needs when it gets down to it, huh?

Kwesi has some great talents in organizing, relating to people, and doing what has to be done. Also, some serious defects, lack of discipline, initiative, confidence . . . all obviously interrelated. That's why I welcome so his new efforts, perhaps he's done some searching and found some real answers. Let's give him a new chance to try anyway. There're a couple other things I wanted to go into but paper's about out. I'll try to keep it fresh 'til Sunday. Oh yes, one is that Francis' friend is no longer here but in my last home. I guess she knows by now, but if not, please hip her so she won't waste a trip. I'll see you later.

Justice in Our Time!
Ernest

•

Retrieve Unit, Texas Department of Corrections
3 July 1973
11:45 PM
To   Mrs. Eva C. McMillan

Hello Maw-Maw!

Today (as well as yesterday!) was quite a day! I saw Dad, San, Kat, and Don on a surprise—really surprising—visit yesterday. I'm sure that by now you have all the news, so I won't go into it all now. Seeing Dad and San (plus a peek at Kat) today was quite a wonderful bonus, too. But the icing on the cake was a letter received today from the Supreme Court of Texas: yes, Zim has finally processed my writ (by denying it naturally!) So, all is very cool with me . . . knowing that in the next months to come, we can expect a steady progress of the writ through Austin and on to the federal level.

It is really great though. Zim has by no means lifted his meager stature in my eyes. He has effectively and sadistically extended my stay in prison (most likely) for a period of 18 months. We can call off any proposed effort or exposé on him for the time being and concentrate our energies on the new problems and confrontations created. Please tell the Georgia "gang" (smiles) the news and I hope it will allow everyone to get out of the dumps on viewing my status.

Everyone has been so beautiful and kind—and I'm not saying anything contrary to that. But, one can't help but feel the sense of helplessness that so naturally comes forth when we try to think in terms of tomorrow in relation to my circumstances. Have no fear, we'll win the battles to come and decisively.

I haven't written Ed because I figured why should another letter from me all of a sudden break the cycle and he finally receive one (smile). No really, I forgot until receiving your letter referring to him today. I knew there was <u>something</u> I was supposed to have done! Is his address still 800 Main Street? If he'd like, I can send him the letter I received from the Tex. S.P. today. If it's any good now, the case number was OC-803 McMillan v Zimmermann. I'll quote the body of the letter (it's dated 2 July 1973): "This court has been advised that your application for writ of habeas corpus has been denied by Judge Zimmermann. Since order has been entered in your habeas corpus proceeding in Dallas County, Texas, as noted above, your petition to the S.P. of Tex for writ of mandamus is rendered moot, and it has been dismissed." (Note: my abbreviations & underlinings.) Please excuse my scratchy writing but I'm writing at a 100 m.p.h.

I also received a letter from John today. I hope he has mine also—he didn't say whether or not he'd received mine. Tell him I'm looking forward to seeing him, also check to see if he received my letter.

There is absolutely no way I can adequately comment on your letter. All I can say is "beautiful!" I'll save my words for Sunday, OK? Oh, you don't have to write Harriette. I heard from her yesterday, finally. If you talk to Kay, tell her I haven't forgotten her and that I'm in good health and all. I'm two letters behind her but I'll catch up in all my letters tomorrow.

It was so great seeing the family. Everyone was so full of life and love. I won't be any good for weeks behind that!

I'll close for now. I'll write again tomorrow with the hopes that you'll receive it by Saturday at the latest. I'm going to try & jot down some do-not-forgets and other last-minute thoughts and things.

Stay as strong & beautiful & wise as you are. Give love to all. I'm writing you tomorrow also.

Your son and comrade,
Ernest

•

Retrieve Unit, Texas Department of Corrections
11 July 1973
7:15 PM
To   Mrs. Eva C. McMillan

Dearest Mother,

First of all, forgive me for not writing any sooner, the fault is all mine
. . . I hope you are able to imagine though how busy and hectic things
have been <u>this</u> week. Really! I received your letter written on Sunday and
found all the photos enclosed. (Now everyone is anxious to hurry up and
see Africa!)

I saw Rep. Eddie Bernice Johnson, Rep. Mickey Leland, and others today! It was truly a historic occasion in the annals of prison reform.
It represents a very small step on the true road to justice and humanity in
the penal system. But, what a great step! ("A journey of a thousand miles
begins with the first step" huh?) A valuable lesson was learned today by
many and I guess I have proved to be one of the most eager students. All
morning long, the radio had been forecasting the event, but when I actually saw and talked to them, I found myself emotionally unprepared for
the impact of it all. Just imagine me in my cell, pacing up and down, and
turning around to see Eddie, Mickey and others standing (with a look
of such concern and determination) right in front of my door. (I can see
now why Joan of Arc, for instance, became such a powerful force to the
French in their wars against the English!) I guess I'll also have to admit
that I've fallen in love again . . . There is just no way possible I could view
her in any amount of objectivity (smiles). I guess enough books have been
written about the attachment of the condemned-and-desperate man to
the high-spirited and principled lady, so much for that for now. (smiles)

I was deeply impressed by Mickey, as well. We would have indeed
undergone some progressive giant steps for us to have such heroic cham-
pions of the people standing tall on the Brazos River Bottom, huh? What
can I say? I hope by now you've talked with Ms. Johnson to know that I

am in good health and the extent of the most productive meeting. By the way, is she widowed, divorced or what? Just for the record is all—ha!

The news carried a report on the 6 PM news; their report was mediocre but I think folks are so hip to such news reports today that they could grasp the meaning of the "unmentioned."

Have you talked with Mrs. Cruz lately? (Oh, I found out today that Ed has finally made the move to Frisco!) Do you think I should get in touch with V & Frank now or follow Marcus' suggestion? I'm anxious to get someone to follow up on it and you know I'm not that choosy especially since my appeal—writ of habeas corpus can hardly be modified. The only problem is to see that the Northern District of Texas gets to act on it as soon as possible. Mickey offered his support on that as well. Beautiful!

Oh yeah, Mrs. Cruz: I'm hoping that you are aware of the statement and that it's proved OK for release. The FBI visited me earlier this week and it looks as though practically every agency imaginable is on the case now. The agent's name is Fred V. Crowley, FBI badge no 53329.

I guess the gang has made it back to Georgia by now, huh? Wasn't that a great visit! Did you and San work out any kind of mutual agreement, or was I being unrealistic in my suggestions? Please let me know. I'm dropping each of them a note tonight. I think Dad has conceded me to be more Partee than McMillan (smiles). For now, I'm Uncle Cecil "all over!"

How are you? Jackie? Everyone? I placed an order for a small fan for my cell. The heat is really becoming intolerable, so it's a necessity rather than a luxury. Did Frances J. see her friend? How is he?

Let me know how things are coming at home. I hope I haven't caused you any worry over my lax writing this week. I knew I would see the Representatives and that they'd let you know how I was, plus there was a lot of work to be done. Tough 'suses! It won't happen again—on my part anyway.

Take care.
Determined to Struggle & Win!
Ernest

•

Retrieve Unit, Texas Department of Corrections
Labor Day 1973
To   Mrs. Eva C. McMillan

Hello Mother,

It was such a great pleasure to visit with you and the "gang" Sunday. It is always such a beautiful and rewarding experience to visit with you all. Shortly after you left, an announcement was made that we would not work today, so I've taken advantage of the day's rest for study and meditation.

The good forces of nature have unleashed a hurricane that is headed almost directly to where we are. It is expected to hit by 6 AM tomorrow; everyone here is cheering her on. I trust Kathy and all will be safe in Houston. The winds will not be of true hurricane force, but for our narrow interests here as slave laborers, no wind is too strong.

Zim's actions are really worrying/frustrating me. It is the most awful feeling to be at his mercy. I never expect "mercy" from foes—a hard-learned lesson—but I have always been in some position to counter, to help myself in some way . . . up until today. It seems to be a game for Perini as well; my life that is. There is no way in the universe that it requires several months to sign a piece of paper! We know it is a hollow excuse to maintain my imprisonment and there should be some way we can combat it.

I view three prospects: (1) for me to go through the Texas Supreme Court again, (2) to try to enlist people like Lip to make Zim's action public knowledge, and (3) to see if someone like the Saint would discuss an unconditional pardon with the Gov. In fact, all three efforts (and more) might be needed: I'm even inclined toward Bro Beasley's suggestion you mentioned Sunday. As far as going to the Supreme Court, well it's the slowest and most ineffectual of the lot. The most they would do is ask Zim in the political fashion has he anything to do with a writ of mine, etc., etc.

The pardon idea is the one I suggested way back last year but no one seemed to think it was enough for them to concern themselves with, outside of lip service. And, for someone to picket Zim's offices, and to hold a press conference to explain why, can be of some effect. As long as Zim's actions are behind-the-scenes machinations then he will continue to treat life indifferently. Yes, I am angry and it is getting hard for me to hear this status. I know you're in quite a strain yourself and have an equal concern about my imprisonment. Some may think that I ought to just sit and wait until June (when the parole board "reviews" my case) before anything should be done. If anyone expresses such to you, I'd view it as a conspiracy to lengthen my stay in prison. If I did live to be eligible for parole in June, I don't see any guarantee or any practical method for preventing them from setting me off a year and to do the same the following year, etc.

Anyway, by June '74, I don't think I'd be too good for much—another permanent injury of the prison factory. These things are real and I hesitate swapping horror stories with you. We need to discuss what needs to be done, rather than why things need to be done. At any rate, we should be beyond that level.

Please discuss the pardon idea with her, Mickey, Marcus, or someone who is in such a category? Perhaps Marcus could help V. find a way to motivate Zim? Maybe you discuss all of these points with Lip with the purpose of him getting an idea of how best to publicly expose the situation. It is time for me to write mucho letters, too.

Has Mrs. Cruz been informed about the 14th? I plan to drop her a line about it anyway. I do hope the site location will be Austin. The security problem is a bogus smokescreen of lies. Just today, 24 such hardlined criminals went to perform in the Muscular Dystrophy telethon. The drill team, that is. They go to Angleton, Huntsville and places around the state. Perhaps, if such knowledge were available to the Legs, they'd easily deny his arguments for what they really are. Wherever it is, I hope we get a good people's representation. Dallas, Houston, etc.

I have to make adjustments in my mailing list. I'm getting Harriette off. Thinking about getting Charlie off also, since he doesn't write anyway. Also, Harry, if he is not coming let me know about his situation. I want to put Jackie & others on. I'm definite (now!) about Charlie and Harriette. I'll do that this week.

I'll write more later. Take care. Thank you for buying the picture. I'm glad you liked it. I know they will also.

Love ya,
Ernest

•

Retrieve Unit, Texas Department of Corrections
11 September 1973
To   Mrs. Eva C. McMillan

Beloved Mother,

Received the two letters you wrote 9/8 & 9/9. They were filled with such understanding, compassion—wisdom that I feel much stronger for them, and ashamed too, that my moment of depression was only a self-pitying one; and not at all warranted when one looks at the more advantageous position we face today (as compared to "yesterday").

We're on the threshold of such great victories! I know that a dampened, remorseful spirit is incapable of being an active part of the triumph, so now I'm deeply engaged in sharpening the instrument within my realm that will be necessary if I am to be anyway, one of the many fibers, of the muscle, that will smash/build in the name of the people. I have learned a great lesson and you are indeed a fine teacher! There is no task or problem too difficult or complex for us to overcome. It is this constant rising up to meet the demands of the fluctuating times that will enable us to carry life forward . . .

I just heard the news of the <u>coup</u> in Chile and what appears to be an army takeover. The enemy didn't deal as nicely and legitimately with Allende as he so persistently dealt with them! Another great lesson, in that we're now able to see so clearly, how foolish it is to try peacefully to build a socialist society, when the bourgeois form of rule remains <u>the</u> rule. How absurd . . . yet, now it is unquestionably clear to the workers and peasants of Chile—and peoples throughout the formalities, rules, niceties, customs—system of the capitalist kind. Allende compromised all substantial principles of the people trying to please, appease the various backward elements. Either he grossly underestimated the power of these forces (the revolutionary impetus) or he <u>over</u>estimated the reactionaries . . . likely, it was both with him. The struggle is not over them. I'm more interested and involved in keeping up with the state of affairs there than ever. Just watch what happens now.

I hope that nothing arises to prevent us from getting to Austin. I hope the Legislators stay on the ball and do not fall for any of those smoke-screen maneuvers that are so abundant to the yokels. I really look forward to it; seeing you and the others as well. Looks like you'll have <u>another</u> long & trying weekend, huh? (Is the press conference planned in Houston for the weekend also?)

Mama, you're really doing it! You didn't have to get copies of the deposit slips made! We're not short around here—they're in the plenty. It's just that ole son of yours, so lazy that he won't send you any, as he ought to be. It seems so . . . like begging and worrying you when I send them in the letters, so I believe I really have a mental block about sending them. If it's not too late—I'll do better (smiles) OK?

No, haven't heard from Dad or San this week, but looking to hear from them in a day or so. I wrote them early last week I believe. Please send me Fe's address. I want to drop her a quick note and let her know my unwavering feelings/intentions toward the status of my son in relation to me/us. I will try to get permission to write her a special letter. Don't forget.

Yes, I'm receiving the *Guardians*. I'm glad Jackie told her of my thirst for books. What books did Neva decide to send, if any? The situation with the family in L.A. What can we do to bring folks closer together there, anything?

How did the conference go with Joe? Sounds like there's some progress when you said he "called" you over the phone! (smiles) Please relay my respect, confidence, and revolutionary faith in him. (What I mean is, let him know that I really look forward to working at his side.) I hope Liz gets well soon.

I'm thinking of getting a copy of my old letter from the Supreme Court along with the writs themselves and going into the federal courts myself. What do you think? I'll need for V to mail me all the materials — the original & amended writ for this to be. Think it's possible to get him to do it. I'll write more later. Take good care.

For our people!
Ernest

•

Retrieve Unit, Texas Department of Corrections
2 December 1973
To   Mrs. Eva C. McMillan

Mother,
Pardon me for not writing any sooner; hung up trying to put a written report together. Oh, well (smiles). Trust you have received one letter from me this week, huh? Rec'd your letters, too, I believe already this past

week. Glad to hear of the fine responses from the people on the upcoming trip. I hope there aren't any changes in dates or postponements.

My concentration and study habits are very poor these days. For the last month or so there have been a few things that I've wanted to deal with but because of upcoming events and general hassles, I've postponed the effort. I keep saying when all this is behind me for a while I'll take a self-inventory to see just what all the "excess baggage" is all about. It may not be excess baggage at all, perhaps I'm short a few necessary items. It's good, regardless though, to take stock periodically of just where you are, where you're going and what can be done to enhance unity (external and internal).

Even that is progress of a sort . . . I can still vividly recall the times I used to ask myself "why me? "or "how come such and such is called for at all." Now, I'm at least beyond questioning commitment in general and wondering how the world got the way it is. Today, I'm standing face to face with a long hard row and trying to better my strokes so as to economize energy/mistakes and put forth the best effort at the same time. I hope that doesn't come off sounding like conceit or even a form of depression on the other hand. I really don't feel it's either.

Hope to see you and the gang soon! Please take care. I know there are some questions and comments I have from your last letter but I'll try to get into that in my next letter. OK? I will write Jackie a note tonight, too.

We welcome struggle in whatever form it assumes. Resistance and progress are Siamese twins, separated only with death . . . and life is struggle.

Ernest

1974

Retrieve Unit, Texas Department of Corrections
9 January 1974

Hello Mother,

Saw Mrs. Cruz [*Frances Cruz, renowned prison rights advocate/attorney*] today! It was a very pleasant surprise visit. Not very much news, but she was most helpful with counsel on legal procedures. She gave criticism on my writ that was most valuable but a little late (alas!), all in all, it was a most welcome visit.

The mail office received four books from International Publisher. I may receive them tomorrow if they meet the "approved list" standards of TDC. I don't know if the books were from you or Nee Nee. I don't recall the name of the fourth book off hand but the ones I recall are *The Unstable Economy* by Victor Perlo, *Selected Works of Marx & Engels* and *Neo-Colonialism* by Kwame Nkrumah. I will let you know if I receive them or not tomorrow.

If you are able to reach EBJ soon (I know how difficult that may be by phone) but find out from her if the Constitutional Convention Energy Crisis et al will mean that the Prison hearings are delayed until springtime or later. OK?

Received the money from San and $20 from W. McMillan—the "W"—is probably a mistake, unless it stands for "We," huh?

I guess Kay, Bob, and Marky made it off all right and are back in California for now, huh? How about Dad? I wonder how his meeting with Zan went. Please let me know.

I'm sorry I didn't write you last night as I had promised. I did write Kat and I didn't want to write you two short notes back to back. I hope Kat contacted you and let you know I was OK on the 8th of Jan. (smiles?)

I felt since I told you in my last letter that I had worked out the "problem" satisfactorily with the keepers that you would be less anxious about my situation. Anyway, the "crisis" I foresaw on visiting day didn't materialize (and won't either).

Are there any events planned in Dallas for Jan 15th MLK's birthday? There was some talk of it becoming a national holiday. Has it? I imagine that there will be TV coverage or memorials around him for that day. The dominant theme/view will be something to the effect that he was a non-violent, peaceful man who had a utopian dream. This is the emasculating service (free of charge) of the capitalist press. It is a shallow, one-sided, and corruptible (corrupting?) presentation of a man who in his very last days made a heroic attempt to propel himself/and the masses of people to a new level of struggle. The press will play that down or more than likely, twist his last month of life into a neat compartment of the most rigid and immovable type.

To them, M. L. King of 1958 is no different from M. L. King of 1968, which is the worst kind of fantasy. It is so vital that we look at the history of the man, his evolutionary journey and his relations with society and trace his very rich growth. It was a process that covers no small or simple amount of ground. This is also the source of my admiration, love, and undying respect for him. It is no easy task to confront yourself, especially in a time when one is riding high on a wave of established acceptance, and say to yourself "say, look what I am about is nowhere close to lifting the weight of oppression that faces my people."

I'm not saying this is the manner he addressed himself but I do believe that he took a deep inner surveillance and a hard honest objective look at the conditions and strategy he had tried to reconcile and say that he was missing the target. He then began to move in a determined fashion to new priorities and questions that he could have evaded or ignored with a "fine" rationale. It is so remarkable that he started on a new trail rather than coast comfortably on the superhighway that had been laid before him. The war in Vietnam, the question of genocide, feeding the poor became his compelling targets. Lurking just below the surface of these questions lay capitalism, racism and imperialism, and their undeniable relationship. I remember him saying that the logical conclusion of racism is genocide and for capitalism, it is war.

Being so firmly against war and genocide as he was in word and deed, the logical development for him was to become firmly anti-capitalist, and, therefore socialist in word and deed. The same is true for Malcolm. I found in re-reading some of his works in Malcolm X Speaks just how close he too was to becoming truly revolutionary. The Assassins cut them off from life and the people physically, because more than anything else Martin & Malcolm were not only swiftly developing into revolutionaries but they were a living theater for the people—a living classroom for they shared their knowledge and understanding with us honestly and unsparingly.

Where they went, we too, as a powerful force, were most certain to go also and not far behind. Martin was a little slower in the aspect of learning, I believe than Malcolm. I guess King was, due to his own conservatism—due to religion most likely. Yet, both were so sincere and honest . . . so brave. And, confident in history, their people and truth that this kind of confidence makes one a slave to the impulse for liberation.

How can one ever abandon struggle when they know that history, truth and yes, time propels them closer and more capable of winning real liberation? If we can strive to be like them just in the respect of self-honesty, what a tremendous surge forward that would be for the whole world of downtrodden men and women. If we could in that way declare ourselves enemies to falsehood, we would at the same time be great servants of truth.

Ernest

P.S.   'scuse my poor writing and mistakes—as always (smiles).

•

Retrieve Unit, Texas Department of Corrections
20 February 1974

Hello Mama,

Received your letter of "Monday afternoon" (18 Feb) just today. Thanks for the wealth of info about the family, V, and all. I haven't written V yet and now I'm glad I haven't because really there's nothing to say. He says the information I am seeking will be a part of the records made available to the court and in the next breath, he says Zim has goofed and has yet to be corrected. I am confused. How can one of his statements be true if the other is supposed to be true too? He is contradicting or I'm missing out on something. I couldn't understand from your letter but would you tell me if the research material that Z. failed to submit to Austin is somehow now a part of the court's records? I will write him if your answer is still unclear—perhaps he hasn't made it plain to you what I'm saying.

Have you learned anything about Joy? I'm concerned about her. Hopefully, you or Kat have reached her or her mother. I wrote Dad tonight . . . finally. My first letter to him since January or since seeing him last. He's probably pretty "swole."

Enjoyed the article on Maiz. Thankx! I can <u>feel</u> why the article had special interest to you: to move from the bowels of the prison system to the height of establishment acceptability is probably a wish you would like to see for me . . . coming from a maternal instinct. (Let me know if I'm wrong). I think one has to flirt with those circles in order to be recognized in the first place. So, I doubt if they'll get <u>any</u> sugarplum visions when looking my way. I don't doubt we need real good folks in those positions; it's just that I'm sure there are plenty of niggers too willing and too capable of filling those kinds of posts. At the same time, they are so, so scarce when it comes to the gut level confrontation points.

I'd like very much (whenever I get out of prison) to fall into an area where I have some resources and the physical setup to work with, but I feel I'm going to really have to scuffle and sweat for such. The Bethlehem Center would be a really beautiful setup to work with if I had freedom to operate and decide about things that go on within it. But, that looks more like a hopeless case considering the conditions in Dallas and among the Methodists (including Zan).

I remember in '71 when I was finally busted, you wrote to me that in a lot of ways you were glad—relieved because you didn't have to worry and go through the sleepless nights 'bout my well-being and whereabouts when I was the "fugitive." That really burned me at first—still smacks a little, too now—but in thinking it over, I accepted your perspective as a mother toward a son. I also remember the letter I rec'd from you that gave me so much encouragement to keep on keeping on a little earlier than that one. I kept that letter and used to read it over and over. It, too, was from a mother to her son but it was acceptance of the circumstances and my choice in it all. Maybe you were just saying that for the morale side, but it was more than that to me.

Do you remember it and how you felt then? One thing that I so truly value from my family but seldom if ever comment about is the support you've shown me. Sometimes, it amounts to a stand of non-resistance that is "we don't like what you're doing but you're doing it and you're a man so we will not obstruct you." Even that is cool. But, my undying hope is that you and the family identify more with the struggle in such terms as it is "us" rather than "he." You see. And to me, that is more the case than ever and I hope it is not simply because of my being in prison and the sufferings here that you are relating to, but rather see this as a continuing part of the very struggle that the whole world is now embroiled in a desperate death-life grip.

I know that it would bring you a kind of peace to know that I'm working on a "safe" job, that I have banker's hours and live in regulated fashion, but I really doubt if this is real peace . . . even in mother-son terms.

I think it is withdrawal and defeat in the fullest sense and that has to generate the worst kind of misery—static misery.

One of the chief supports of this system and therefore a maintainer of exploitation, is the very able and gifted persons like Maiz who peddle their wares and soul to the keeper for his trinkets and plaudits . . .and for comforts sake [personal comfort] it's just a small, small splinter to them but for the advancing people, it is a whole tree that has been carved and made into poisonous <u>spears</u> that point at their/our throats now.

Let us strive for the unhesitating acceptance of our own to our own . . . Serve the people!

Ernest

•

Retrieve Unit, Texas Department of Corrections
9 March 1974

Hey Mama Mack!

Yes, I received the affidavits—you all are certainly on the ball! It was a most pleasing surprise and you can bet I really need M. Farrah's statement. So far, it seems I'll have eight "bits" of exhibits to include as evidence. Most of it is to show how the courts in Texas have abused my writ through delays and downright obstruction. Don't tell V—but I shall use one of his letters. The other evidence will be M. Farrah's statement and the newspaper articles if I ever get them.

As I said in my last letter, I wrote V. about sending them as well. It was so timely and considerate to receive the affidavits. Legal Services can say for sure that they performed <u>one</u> great service—for sho (smiles).

I've been thinking about the nature of the critical stage we are in now. The American system has virtually placed <u>post</u>-conviction efforts for justice in a dark shadow of oblivion in the minds of the public. In reality, the writ of habeas corpus is righteously known as the "Great Writ." It is perhaps the greatest single tool for resolving or overcoming injustice that courts, police, agents and political conspirators have leveled against persons. I think it is not accidental that so many people are completely unaware of it, and/or its value to those who have been victimized by the legal machinery.

It is not rare, in the least, for folks to regard the conviction and sentencing as the "end of the road" for their friends or relatives who've stood trial, but it is also frequent that one finds the court system inclined to abuse the writ (and the writ process). These two kinds of daily occurrences go hand-in-hand; one act could not exist without the other—and vice versa. So today, it has come to the level of impotence. Judges now can deny writs without one single explanation. They are allowed every conceivable discretion and most of their power lies in their discretion. For example, the strongest kind of real terms set up for the Courts to follow is "may" (the Court may this or may that) while we the victims of the court) "must" this and "must" that and to the very letter too, or another discretion arises for the courts. The discretion to deny every effort of the victim

I think the only way one can combat these "discretions" is to place post-conviction efforts for relief in the same light that the trial, arrest, and other phases of "justice" (ha!) are now in. This "light" is the public eye. To the courts, the public eye is either a curse or a way out. Too often, it is a way out because "crime in the streets" and the demands for "law and order" has cheapened life and made such "rights" (like freedom from illegal search and siege) of the people, just empty phrases. However, we've seen how the public eye can be a "curse" to the courts because it forces them to have respect/recognition to its phases, e.g. A. Davis, Lee Otis, B. Seale et al.

I want to talk to you about the move. I didn't mean to get into it so. Anyway, I need to think more about it because I feel like conditions have changed greatly from the days when Angela was on trial and therefore tactics must change too. I don't think it is fitting for today to have some folks stand in front of a courthouse and say "free so and so!" (period!)

Before I go, let me say that I rec'd the photo of the clan—it's a nice flick. So many Partees together at once! (laughs).

Glad my letter arrived in time to help keep the phone bill down! I'll do better. My vigilance has been deplorable, not to mention the human value of a letter! Oh, Aunt Gwen's ring will be ready when you visit next week, OK. The prison bus inspired by Mickey Leland and others came in today and was such a tremendous sight-act! It's good to know that Dallas has finally joined the other areas and I feel it will be a big success. It has opened new possibilities for so many men-people they thought they would never see again in years or see again ever; they now will be able to visit. It's been a long time coming, huh?

I plan to write EBJ about it. I'm certain Dallas will see they'll need another bus before long . . . I believe dust can absorb more water than in equal weight of say, terry cloth (just a hunch). What I'm trying to say is, you all have met a very real need . . . ain't enough words. Please supply me with the schedule and the departure point. One day we'll all know that today's deeds are but a mini fraction of what an organized people can do!

Ernest

•

Retrieve Unit, Texas Department of Corrections
13 March 1974

Dear Mother,

I want you to let me know where Glenn [*Felicia's brother*] is exactly so I can try to see to it that he's all right. OK? Say, I think Ohene and I have shared similar histories on the pneumonia thing. Wasn't I about three or four when I came down with it? I hope he is better.

I see where some Skyline students are suing the principal for violation of their civil rights by not allowing speakers of their choice to address them as well as denying placing certain posters on the wall, including mine. Judge Hill seems to be the rightful predecessor of Estes, so I don't think he'll rule favorably . . . it would really be a contradiction for him to sentence me to 3 years and to "allow" the students to utilize my poster in the school. He is <u>consistently</u> unfair, so easy to predict.

No, I haven't seen or heard the news that pinpoints the FBI as conspirators for activist organizations' destruction. When you get the complete list—I'm sure it will be lengthy! Let me know more about SNCC's status. <u>We</u> all know of their (FBIs) real function as the states police— gestapo. Just looking over the history of Dallas SNCC alone makes their true purpose and intent very plain—<u>search out and</u> <u>destroy</u> all threats or potential threats to the rule of the financial—military aristocracy.

Mama, I don't think "letters to the court" is an effective route. The <u>content</u> of approach has to be from the community(ies) but I just can't fathom the <u>form</u> of their action. There has to be a rekindling of fire; and the approaches that have been successfully used around the country as late as '72 & '73 are now (to me) obsolete. Things have changed so rapidly—and I think the apathy and indifference that we experience around us is the result of these swift changes rather than the cause of inactivity. I think it is a natural feeling for humans to withdraw or be apathetic when yesterday's solution is now today's problem.

This is about, in a nutshell, what things are for us today. Helplessness is the root of it all in the face of these mighty and sweeping changes. For example, on the worldwide level, very few people have been able to perceive/explain correctly what is really going on by the "big power" changes in alliances. Yesterday, the USSR was the "Red Menace" now they are "partners in peace." Real pressures and force brought this about, rather than some individual's invention; while <u>we</u> are unable to make corresponding shifts in relations to meet the new needs because we can't see what it is that's really shaping up. We love to adapt and deal with the new and rapidly changing conditions around us. If we don't, we are out of touch with the world around us; in that state of mind, we are subjects rather than agents for change—incapable of resolving anything beyond the automatic everyday situations. Pretty soon, <u>even that</u> becomes a difficulty! So, we have to continue to make analysis of change. Sometimes it calls for minor alterations of forms and eventually the content of the thing (or process) becomes totally new.

Even as I write, my letter becomes old history. It's a <u>race</u> to stay in correspondence with one's self, his surroundings. We'll always be a step or so behind because it takes time for the mind to reflect and for that reason there is no precise/exact knowledge. And so it goes with tactics. For every given situation, there is a proper/correct offense and defense. It is up to us to understand the situation and to build in <u>direct</u> relation to it. That is the overall lesson I learned from the book that was returned to you recently. To me, the subject of guerrilla warfare was just a forum from which this principle (of dealing with every situation) could be explained and understood. I hope you will read it and in <u>that</u> light, for it opens up the mind to so many possibilities about life in general. It will help shed light on the fact of why a "crisis" is a danger and an opportunity <u>at the same time</u>.

I hope by the time I see you I will have worked up some ideas about this new situation with the courts and freedom. So far no luck, but it will be helpful to discuss it with you. Two heads are better than one. We will come up with the opportunity out of the present danger; I have no fear.

Will close for now—thanks to the "bad" weather down here I was able to sit down and write you early because we were forced not to work today due to the conditions—rain, beautiful rain. (Rain also helps the weeds along, ugh!) But, so far so good.

Take good care. My love and best wishes to all our friends. Tell Jackie I'm looking for that letter (smiles). Kiss Yiki for me. A salute to the Skyline students! Dare to win!

Ernest

•

Retrieve Unit, Texas Department of Corrections
6 April 1974

My beloved mother,

So happy to hear from you, as always . . . you don't realize (probably) how much I value your messages.

Things are going well except that today I had an unexpected surprise from the courts (the federal court in Dallas). They have appointed Perini to represent me! Isn't that great? I was prepared for a longer wait on their decision to appoint counsel and that really caught me by surprise. I have just finished writing V. and I informed him that Marcus (more on him later!), John, Jordan and Bobby C. have all expressed a real willingness to be of help. I am anxious to get started on the work in preparation for the hearing, though no date has yet been set. I want V. to make efforts to have me in DCT <u>soon</u> so that we can coordinate things better and I can get busy with getting the needed witnesses, evidence (that we require so badly).

I need you to help push V along on this as he may think otherwise about it (as he so often manages to do!). Whatcha' think. The whole process is a natural one of everyday things so I don't foresee any difficulties even from V. When counsel and client are so far apart as we are and a hearing is upcoming, it is a simple routine as I understand it for the attorney to take the initiative by approaching the judge.

I didn't know that the tornadoes struck Alabama. In fact, my reaction to the news was just a tsk-tsk-tsk until you told me that Dallas County was one of the stricken areas. I'll get off a letter to Bettie/Angie tonight, while hoping they are all unaffected by the storms.

Jackie must have had a premonition about the $16 for the artist being arrested and may be in another area soon. I guess it would be best for her to send it on to me and I'll try to make the arrangement from here. I'm glad she didn't send it as originally planned or it would have been a gift to him rather than wages. (ha!) By Jackie having the money, does that mean that she has already received her income tax refund? I haven't received your money order yet but I'll probably receive it Monday. I'm sorry you have still been unable to buy the ring yet. I was under the impression you had purchased it. Now I know why the dude won't even speak to me. Oh well, I'll explain it to him . . . but no need to apologize.

Say, have you heard any news about Harry's address? I wrote him and haven't gotten a kick back on it. I'm concerned because I believe apartment people don't bother to return the letter to the postman if the letter is not theirs. Also, I'm almost positive Harry said he is living in a "house" now and that he just moved. If you hear from Faye, please verify the address. OK? It's no need to call her for this (no rush) perhaps you could write her.

My Uncle Cecil is t-o-u-g-h! I'm really glad to hear he's getting up and around.

Scarlet fever? That is very serious—and I hope Kat went to the doctor to check it out. From what I understand, it is highly communicable. It could even be that the "cold" she was suffering with was an advanced stage of the Fever. Hope not, but I'm glad you suggested she see a physician right away.

I hope Fe and Ohene make it to Dallas as planned. If so, I'll have a far better chance of seeing him, as there is a good possibility I could be in DCJ next month. It'll be great for all of us as you won't have to be making any of these great expeditions down for a while (and maybe never again, huh?).

That's too hard about Marcus! Let's see, he is running against Ragsdale, huh? Well, from here it seems as though Rags is doing very little. I'd hate for this to be neutralized in the whole thing simply because Rags played a song dedicated to me at some affair . . . Let's feel no sense of duty to him for something like that. What did you tell Marcus? If you haven't reached him yet, I think you ought to come out for one of them soon. As I said before, let it be based on their stance/principles rather than how you may feel about them. As for me, I feel more of an identity with Marcus and it was impressive for him to refuse the city judgeship that Asinine Allen (the next Mayor of Dallas) offered him.

It wouldn't be such a terrific decision to make if we weren't so conscious that the outcome will have a big meaning on future Black, local politics and that these two men have been of rare quality compared to the shady Black politicians we have been completely bombarded with. Whoever you support, ought to have made a solid commitment to the things (some of the things) you're involved with like the rights of prisoners, anti-repression etc., etc. If you haven't contacted Marcus yet, see if he is really planning to develop & work with EBJ on these projects. We already know where Rags has been on these issues like all issues (East Texas).

Do you see any possible means to excite the community into moving toward helping me to win freedom? I think a great determinant (and possibly the only determining factor) in regards to a positive outcome of my case in the courts will be a politically charged atmosphere that is pro-justice for me. There is such a hard shell around the heart of the community, thanks to the repressions, disappointment in leaders, and distractions, that I am still at a loss of a way(s) (a spark) to arouse the community to action. I think it's very nearly time to raise the call for support and I feel we need some new methods for doing so.

As far as Black Dallas politics goes, it is always the same old folks who make up the tiny mix of activists Bell, Gilliam, Lip, Stover, Conrad, etc. and each of these individuals you find over & over again contained to a small unimaginative area of activities with a seemingly disinterested community as their stage of performances. I say "seemingly disinterested" because this to me is only a surface picture of the real condition. Beneath this surface appearance is a mighty volcano, teeming ready to be tapped, and its energies to be raised to a state of mighty production.

I saw how Frankie W. moved an even more cynical population to resolute action and that is encouraging and the type of needed sparks that Dallas needs. And, she is just <u>one</u> independent individual with confidence in the needs of the time as well as others. I think we should try and generate a similar, if not greater, enthusiasm, and sustain it. Ignite and drive! Ignite, not from invoking sympathy, but a burning intolerance for these abominable acts of injustice. And drive. Right now, I'm just spinning my wheels (smiles) unable to find the needed traction! I'll keep searching and in the meanwhile, I would appreciate your thoughts on the matter. OK?

Give my love to Jackie. Tell her I'm looking forward to hearing from her. A kiss to Yiki. Love & Power to you. I'll be writing again soon.

With a revolutionary embrace,
Ernest

P.S. Ask Jackie to mail that money order off to me tonight so I can withdraw it at the next pay period and in time for Angie's birthdate, OK?

•

Retrieve Unit, Texas Department of Corrections
23 April 1974

Hello Mother,

I received notice today that I will be graduating on the 23rd of May (a Thursday). Ceremonies such as they are, will be held at Clemmons. I believe you'll be receiving an invite pretty soon.

It's a shame that I would only be allowed two guests and only from among those on my list! I want Jackie to be there and I was thinking that Dad and Kay would still be around the area and how great it would be to have a family affair out of it all . . . but that is not permissible. "Only two" they say, so I invited you (of course!) and Kathy so she could attend another exercise, but this time as a member of the audience (smiles). It was infuriating to have to be limited to such a compressed list and I hope Jack (et al) will pardon me for failing to include them again! Let me know if you and Kat will be able to be there.

Received your 4/19 letter yesterday and I guess you must have gotten one from me today huh? What on earth is Harriette doing? Is she visiting Dallas, planning to stay, or what? I don't think she'll have any success in getting permission. You know how things are with the bureaucrats down here! You should have forewarned her and saved her some time and energy. The only thing I can think of is that she can come down with you and Vickie Johnson when you all come next week to visit. That is, if she is still in town. Vickie is just a friend and wouldn't mind at all.

I see Harriette is still the master politician with her calling, visiting you and Jack and all—I know she'll have some allies in her camp next week (ha!). But then, she was always your favorite wasn't she (smiles). I mean, isn't she? I'm halfway kidding really (just halfway though) because she always talks and asks about you and Jackie. But, there is no doubt in my mind about her "political ability." I've gotten all stirred up inside and I do hope she makes it down . . . it's always been an incurable malady of mine—Harriett, that is (smiles). So much for that!

I want you to know that the McMillan family is officially dubbed & defined as "all communists," every one of them. Really! Such labels incensed me as my first reaction. I didn't appreciate the manner in which these germs go around doing their best to poison and erode peoples' minds, but after thinking about it all, I feel like they have, in reality, presented me with a fine award. Their definition of a communist is one who wants and works for all the people "having the same." In the least, such an activity as that is a most noble one indeed, and one I'd give my life toward! So, I'm not upset over their vile attempts, for more than anything else their penny ante attempts help to make more popular and prestigious that which is so vague in people's minds. If a bloodthirsty, savage germ has enemies, you can't help but wonder how many droves of good folks would want to be friends with that "enemy." And so much for that and for now only.

I'm to see the parole counselor tomorrow afternoon . . . the same one you talked to briefly a few months ago. I'm sure he is going to want to have the info on the job offers, etc. It caught me by surprise as I was beginning to think I wouldn't see him at all, just the interviewer from Austin next month. But he's to interview me tomorrow and I'll give him all I can . . . I want you to forward that information on to me as soon as you can because I'm sure he just wants to get my file in shape for the interview OK? It doesn't call for a telegram or anything but when you get it send it to me. (Hopefully before the 1st of May.)

Still no letter from EBJ yet! Didn't you say she already was supposed to have written me?

Any word about Eunice, yet.

You know (I think I mentioned it in my last letter) I had to start all over with the gift for Angie, as the artist was transferred. I have another friend putting a portrait together but I haven't had a chance to really talk with him. What I'm wondering is would you bring some extra cash down with you when you visit? Something like $10.00 maybe. I'm going to try to see if he could have it ready by then and I'd save time by getting you to pick it up and mail it to her. Robert Michael (the painter) says it takes him 4 or 5 days to complete one. I don't know even if he's started on it yet, let alone able to finish it in time . . . but just in case he does, I hope you'll be able to pick it up for me. That's why I want you to have an extra ten dollars or so. By the way, things look like it most likely won't be ready.

It's really good to know Kay will be down. If you hear from her, see if she'll have time to visit me and if so, if she'll require a special visit or not. She'll have to write the Warden here if she will be visiting during the week or on one of my off weeks for visits, OK? The same is true for Dad too.

This month is really scooting on by—I hope the next three or four will go even faster—those will be some important ones too. Maybe in three or four, the address of mine will be different—absolutely different!

Well, I'll close for now. I'm still working (cough!) on those three Book reports; would you believe I have two to go still? Well, would you believe two and a half? How about two and three-quarters left to do? Well, by the time you receive this, I will have knocked one of them out, at least.

I see Ranger defines himself as being the moderate and Kirk the conservative and Ragsdale the liberal. Kirk is certainly dead! And I wish I could be as definite about R&R as I am about Kirk. Their campaigns are virtually personality campaigns. Go with the one who makes the commitments you require and good luck! When is the primary, the 8th?

See you soon! I love ya'. In the struggle, your son,
Ernest

•

Retrieve Unit, Texas Department of Corrections
12 May 1974

Dearest Mother,

It is amazing how incredibly petty and technical these yokels can get toward things that are ordinarily human! I am so humiliated and angry at how you and the rest of the family were treated yesterday. Their caveman acts will not go without end or unchallenged, I promise. No act of theirs goes unrecorded or forgotten!

I'm glad you like the painting of Angela! I wanted to keep it myself (smiles). If you'll send me a photo of you (larger than wallet size), I'll ask Mike to paint one of you. I eventually hope to have one for every member of the family made (sounds like egoism huh? smiles). I need one large enough so he can work up a portrait out of it, OK?

I wrote Kat tonight a belated congratulation for her great achievement. I think you deserve a good portion of the salutes upon her commencement into life as a professional—just think, a teacher!

It was good to see you all today. Everyone looked so good to me! Please tell Bob and Kay hello for me (It seems Bob and I have been confined to <u>waving</u> at each other for too long!) Also, Aunt Mildred. I'm glad she liked the ring and I hoped it fits her well. Also, for Uncle Cecil—I know how much he wanted to be down for the graduation. Dad sounded and looked—even acted (smiles) as best I've seen him in a long time. I told him and San to kiss you, Kay and Mildred for me. By proxy kiss for your birthday, and for just being you. San looked as pretty as ever and I really was overjoyed with her presence! I've got so much "mushy" stuff I could say but I'll refrain for the time being. I feel as though it's a New Year beginning and like we are all on the eve of a very great and ever so bright future. Full steam ahead!

I just received notice that I am to be interviewed by a representative of the Parole Board tomorrow! So, by the time you get this letter, we can begin our countdown on the news of their decision. It usually takes about 6 weeks to hear something so that will be around the first of July or so. I'll keep pressing on my writ in the federal court as that is uppermost in my mind—real freedom—no strings attached. I can't help but wonder as to what will be their decision. I wish you could relate to EBJ and M. Leland what's happening so they can do their thing—whatever it is. Really, I can't help but think we've already done about all that can be done and that the major portion of the work on my habeas corpus and parole plan has been done. Am I getting complacent?

So good you talked with the lady from San Antonio and I hope something will be done to be of real help to her and family. Perhaps, Mr. & Mrs. Sullivan can be of real use here as they are from San Antonio and have such great contacts. Let me know what cha' think?

What happened to the bus from Dallas? A bus came down today but it was from Ft. Worth. There were many sad faces around today as I came back to my wing from the visit. Several had strongly anticipated seeing their mothers/wives, kids, etc. on this day.

Hope you received my card and can find it in your heart to forgive me for letting your birth date slip me by. I'm so sorry and you must not let me off the hook so easily by saying it was nothing, OK?

Give my love to Jackie, Yiki and all! I will write Kate and San tonight at the Houston address if I can beat the lights . . .

I'll close for now but I'll write soon to let you know how the interview went.

Love ya,
Ernest

•

Retrieve Unit, Texas Department of Corrections
27 May 1974

Hello Mother,

Trust you made it safely back to "D" and that the ride back on the bus wasn't too tiresome a journey. If I can just possess a fraction of the stamina and energy you exert I will be able to accomplish much when I am released. How do you do it? Really!

It's easy for me to understand why a lot of people around here seem to think I am of wealthy folks instead of the poor, struggling people we are. I believe they think you must ride here in air-conditioned chauffeured Rolls or own a private jet to visit, as you do and to be so lively. I think too of the endurance & stamina & determination you showed in caring for Mother Dear as you did, while holding down a tiresome job and with little thanks and zero compensation.

I admire you so, and I am so indebted to you for so much. I am so fortunate, so "rich" in so many ways, to have such beautiful loved ones and good friends. I have learned so much about real heroism and bravery from others in these past years that I had to say so at the risk of sounding foolish.

I love you. Have a good day!

Your son,
Ernest

P.S. Love to Jackie & Yiki

•

Retrieve Unit, Texas Department of Corrections
16 July 1974

I am in receipt of your 7-15-74 letter today. It is highly unusual for me to have in possession a letter from you written the day before, but it is just fine with me!

I hope you'll be making it down to Austin. I'd love to see you! Trust everything goes as you expect it. I hope there are no unforeseeable but yet predictable tricks from the dirty tricks section this time as before. The news of the hearing was a real surprise to me—it's hard to believe that it's finally soon to be a reality. Will the hearing be for just Saturday? I had the impression from Janet that it was a two-day thing Fri & Sat but you seem to imply that it's for a Saturday only. Perhaps, there will be an occasion and opportunity for us to visit. Sorry EBJ won't be there. Really, need her presence, too!

I'm hoping you told San & Kat about it. I'm not writing them tonight on the hunch that you did. Hope they will be able to make it. You are really on the ball and I have a treasured picture in my mind of you on the phone, at the courthouse and just rapping to people in general about the hearing. All in the style, a la Eva!

I'm trying to prepare for this thing. What I have already are some notes, descriptions of a particular institution, but it seems obsolete now.

I hate to play it by ear, when time is so precious . . . It's time for an economical (well organized, and concise) statement. I'll try to do what I can, recognizing the needs as best I can. You probably know that what I say will have a regressive effect on my status here as well as with the Board in Austin. It's kind of scary to think about, knowing plenty of effort will be made to make me regret that day. I choose to go on with the show.

Guess I'm not good at much else besides being a ham and playing on the team that appears to be the disadvantaged. Pray you're with me . . . certain you are though I know you are seriously/somber. That's the way I will be. I guess our slogan after this weekend ought to be "V" now more than ever (smiles). Perhaps if others before me had made a stand despite the immediate costs, I wouldn't even be facing such a situation at all. With me in it, I think of the possibility that someone else may be freed from such a wretched choice, damned if I do & damned if I don't. For our Ohene and all the Ohenes!

Thank you for the explanation of the Board's statement to Kay & Bob. For a minute, in your letter I thought you were convinced you'd already related EBJ's report to me in an earlier letter (which was not the case). I was relieved when you wrote anyway about it, though you felt I might have already known. The Board is up to some jive flimflamming! I have been in Class III from the case at the Walls in '73 but I lost no good time because I never had any in the first place. One must be in TDC for a period of time before he's eligible for good time, and at that time, I hadn't fulfilled the waiting period.

I stayed in Class III a little over six months and the Warden at Retrieve recommended my being lifted out of it (as was done). I received a letter from the Walls Record Office shortly afterward informing of my being placed back in Class I and that "zero good time was restored" because zero (000) good time was even taken." I have that letter somewhere in my records and I'll start trying to dig it up. The board has in effect let me off for two months and not just changed my review date out of some technical qualification I failed to meet. Why was I interviewed in May then, if my review month was/is August then my initial interview is to be the immediate, preceding month (July)? I saw the Parole Examiner in May because June is my review month.

All they're doing is trying to camouflage the fact that they have already reviewed my case and made a decision, which was to deny me parole for two months at that time to come before them again. They're stalling for time. I firmly contend they're doing so because of the July hearings (this weekend) in Austin. They still want to have a sword dangling over my head to regulate my mind and communications to the committees is all they are about. It would be an embarrassing and awkward maneuver to pull, if they suddenly granted me parole say July 7th and revoked it July 20th. When in the interim, the only "bad behavior" (or whatever they'd call it) would have been my participation in Legislative Hearings, you dig?

They, rather than do such a shallow and indefensible thing, cooked up a way to have me reviewed after the hearings. Then everything becomes easier for them to carry out and defend. This is only more fuel for the fire.

I'll try to infuse these facts in my presentation. What do you think? Please let me know if what I'm saying is unclear. I don't want to have anything left hanging in your mind about it, no room for misunderstanding. OK? We can expect such action (dirty tricks) by the keepers but that doesn't mean they go uncontested.

I deeply appreciate the Saints' letter to the Governor. She is so wonderfully energetic and knows how to direct her energy to the fullest. Don't you think so?

I heard from Dad today—in a philosophical and cheerful mood. Also heard from Kat & San yesterday. Can't help but think you were instrumental for San's letter (smiles).

I'll close for now; still have some work to do! Looking forward to seeing you soon and the possibility of embracing you with all my love.

Your son,
Ernest

•

Retrieve Unit, Texas Department of Corrections
31 July 1974

Hello mother,

Received your Sunday evening letter a few minutes ago. Hopefully, you got mine the following day. I feel you should have received mine by then at the very latest.

The Austin trip and presentation for it set me behind on my studies and writings. As you can see, I'm still behind on my letter writing because I've only written you once since then, I believe. (I don't wish to sound as though I am offering that as an excuse, though I do feel "guilty" about not writing.) I am trying to fight off my desire to find an excuse and the unhealthiness of feeling guilt at the same time. This "fighting off" that I'm talking about is not a very descriptive word of what I'm actually trying to say. It's more an attempt to come to terms with my real feelings (and to be honest) and to accept this as being me without any shades of remorse.

You are wondering now what in the world is with me and what am I saying. Also, you may be thinking what brought all this on. Let me try to explain: for some while now I have been haphazardly trying to deal with me personally. You know, for a cat pushing thirty, I know little about my real feelings. I have really refused to allow a conscious knowledge of this inner person. I really want to be able to truly relate to people, to be close, and aware of others and self. I want to be capable of living life being on top of my own feelings, free of games and secret feelings. I have come to feel the need for building lasting relations with others on a "for real" basis. I want to go through life this way rather than be a little man in a thick shell cold, unfeeling, and estranged from the things and persons around me.

One big help and a big stimulus to me in admitting this need and admitting my failings in this vital area, has been the Social/Psychology course. We've been doing some reading as I have mentioned before. Such books as "Interaction Ritual," "On Becoming a Person," "The Games People Play" have put things in an unavoidable perspective. What I mean is, what I've secretly thought, randomly worked at, and unconsciously pursued have been brought before me in bright and crystal-clear terms through these studies. Not that I have discovered some formula or some mysterious method for such; just that now some of the things I have pondered/lacked are being questioned and dealt with in an enlightening detail through the class, and the books we're studying in it.

It is most helpful, but it is also so fluid and new to me that I have put off writing letters some time because I really didn't know what to say . . . I didn't know just where I was exactly or if I could write anything that would make sense to you or Dad, San, Kat, etc. while I was looking inward. Don't think for a minute that I am writing now because every-thing is behind me or that I have resolved anything monumental. (smiles). It's just that now I have made enough sense of things to say exactly and out loud what in tarnation I am trying to do.

Austin was quite an experience for me! For the first time in my life (that I am aware of) I actually listened to the questions from the group and then answered just on whatever came out. In a situation like that and before now, I would've been half-listening to their ques-tions and running my computer off in my mind, searching for the "cor-rect" response at the very same time. This time, I was less conscious of myself and attempting to be right there—hearing the sounds, watch-ing the gestures, digging the emotional levels and actually experiencing them—in a conscious way. Of course, I stuttered some and had some messed up sentence structures & sentence orders, and may have said the same thing over several times, but at least I was there and I was in contact with the things around me more than I've ever been in my life. I guess I was on pretty safe ground in the first place and may not have risked much by attempting what I did because all the questions and answers were of my direct experiences.

I wonder what the question & answer period would have been like if it was of another nature? I really felt good about what I was doing, inside myself. I expected some mistakes and bad grammar & some incoherent phrases but since this is a first attempt, it is to be expected. I feel as though the less self-conscious I can become, the more feeling I can sense, and the more aware I am of the things around me, well I believe this is to become more of a person. I forced nothing, everything just, well, everything just came on out. I couldn't believe that I was going to let go and rely upon whatever was there inside me. I wasn't sure how it was going to go, or come out at all, but now I have more confidence and reliance upon myself as a result. I have been missing so much and still there is so far to go!

I know you are hating to go back to work after such an enjoyable vacation. Did you really enjoy it? I hope so; I know getting the rest and the time to yourself was a drastic change in the daily routine.

Hope you'll find San to be easy to live with. She is sort of nervous about things, wondering if she's really wanted and afraid she's really wearing out her welcome. I believe that when she gets there and gets to know you, she'll laugh at how silly it was to feel the way she did. I can imagine what she's going through though being away from home and actually living with persons who entered her life so uniquely and who were complete strangers not long ago.

I'm glad you'll be coming down this Sunday. I was hoping that San was coming with you. We have much to talk about and David and I would really just be going through some formalities and courtesies. I hope you all will be able to re-arrange things and perhaps he & I will visit some other time. My visits are so precious to squander on social niceties (sp?) If it's unclear what I'm saying, I will say before a wrong impression is formed that I like David and think he is a good person. We don't have too much to say to each other and I think we require different circumstances to get to know each other, as we should.

I'll close for now. Forgive me for being so slow in writing. I'm OK. Thinking of you and wishing all the best to you as always.

Take good care Mama Mack. Have any word from any of your grand-chilluns? Stay wonderful.

Your son,
Ernest

•

Ramsey Unit, Texas Department of Corrections
27 August 1974

Greetings mother!

Happy to hear from you as I was beginning to worry if all was not well with you in Dallas since it's been a week (almost) since hearing from you last. Reading your letter was double enjoyment then because I was afraid; I might have been misunderstood in my last letter. It was double enjoyment because I was relieved to hear from you (and to know I had no cause for alarm). And to know that I am accepted and understood as well. (I had a slight suspicion that could be the case before receiving your letter—smiles.)

Perhaps my upcoming anniversary has something to do with my self-inventory, but conditions other than that are important too. One of the things I learned this summer, for instance, is that the creative mind continually finds it surprising and wonderful that a world even exists and that of all the possibilities we have the order, arrangements, and compositions that we do. I laughed at such upon first hearing this because I've been so concerned with what is, "I've detracted from what could be" in the world. Mr. Wegman, the UH teacher, said he felt even "great" men like George Washington must have wondered before the day of a battle just what in the hell he was doing as head of the Continental Army and how did he become such.

I've thought about it since then and now I'm coming to realize some of what he was getting at . . . A person needs to pause and look at himself or herself and see what it's about and what direction he's traveling. Freedom is just as much a part of the forces of life as necessity. A person has freedom to choose the path to a real extent just as necessity exists to an important degree to shape the path and the nature of the choice. Before now, I've looked overwhelmingly at the necessity side and neglected the freedom side.

I'm far from being the creative mind or as important to history as a Washington but I think it is important to take good hard looks at things—not only at the external but the inner and not only the necessity side for the chance or freedom side too—from time to time. I think the world has grown too much, is far too complex, and contains too many levels of life, to allow a person to go through it really involved and desirous of making fundamental changes in it and to be so shallow or one-sided as to be about one race or one tactic or one goal.

Well, as far as that goes, perhaps the world has always been too complex and large for such! But, certainly today, modern man has to be flexible, imaginative, and undogmatic as well as being disciplined, realistic, and partisan. It seems contradictory and a state not possible for one soul, but for two, but I say it's possible for one to be about all these things at the same time. A person with some answers for the present world situation has to be a person who's asked some damn good questions too, huh? I think that a firm captain of a ship must also be loose enough to look at all the alternatives, and be flexible, too.

Well so much for that for the time being . . . another day has come its 28th of August—I got pulled away from my letter listening to my cell partner who likes to rap only once in a while but when he does it means good-bye to everything else I had intended to do otherwise. In the meanwhile, another letter from you has arrived, along with one from San and Kay. Bingo! So tonight, I'm pressing to answer each of them and let nothing sidetrack me.

One fact, you can get more accomplished (as my mother) and I'd prefer that. This is what I called myself saying in my last letter and I'm so sorry I led you to believe otherwise by not being clearer—I will be more careful in the future. If I had been more concise and to the point I believe we would all be in full knowledge of their decision and at least we would be aware to that extent. It would be a great relief to me to know and I wish you'd do it as soon as possible. I'll leave it up to you who to talk with; it would be a simple thing even for a clerk to relay to you. It's like asking Ma Bell what is your bill this month?

I'm sure they've decided something already and I do not treat your bill lightly this month. I do not treat lightly your willingness and desire to do more but I don't think there's anything required of us now but to find out just what my status is—did I or did I not make parole? Plain and simple.

OK? I believe any additional tactics at this time would be an overkill so to speak and with you, EBJ, Al and Farmer (et al) beautiful efforts to date are sufficient.

Saturday, a subscription from *The Call*, the October Leagues newspaper, was denied to me. The paper looked like a good one and the denial here was sure proof that they must be saying something. I appealed to the Director but I think the issue is "moot" with them. I'm so tired of hassles like these; they rob a person of so much strength if he lets them. I think Harry subscribed to *The Call* for me, and I'll write him soon. If you hear from him before I do, let him know. I believe you say he has a new address. Do you know it yet?

I learned that the Vocational Rehabilitation outfit sees to it that ex-cons are financed to further their education. If the SMU scholarship falls through or is insufficient, I will look to the TRC for aid. I believe they're the same ones who assisted in getting Kathy started at U of H.

Things are picking up at my job here. The year-end inventory is due in soon and it seems like I'm responsible for compiling it. It looks like a headache but I have from now to Sept 20th to complete it. There is a lot of equipment and materials—plumbing, electrical, lumber, concrete, sand, asphalt, bolts to bulldozer's—everything one can think of related to construction. The inventory will not interfere with writing and school-work because I leave all the headaches from the job right there. But, it will definitely interfere with my day dreaming time (smiles).

I'd like to say again how I appreciate your insight and wisdom in response to my kooky letter last time. Thanks! You know I was thinking it is impossible for me to exist without you! It's a simple/profound truth. You are irreplaceable; in the truest sense, we owe you the world! I hope the Labor Day traffic isn't too rough to be out driving such a distance in. It may be best to wait for the following week to come down. What do you think? I hope you get this letter in time or that you've already considered the hassles involved for an expedition to South America (South Texas) this weekend.

Karen brought back to my mind some fond memories in her letter today when she said she'd like to cook me one of my favorites, meatloaf with mushroom sauce. Remember that, ha! I had completely forgotten my attempts at cooking around the house—real fiascos—but, maybe not as bad as some of Dad's. Remember his strawberry pie no one ate and those breakfasts of his that went into the garbage. A few did turn out win-ners but were few and far in between.

I noticed your liberated "title" on the envelope. Hey! Hey! (Smiles). Mom, I asked you a couple of times before without response—once when I was in DCJ and again in a letter from Kansas, just what do you want most out of life, what would you like to do and what would make you happiest? I wish you'd share your feelings on this with me. I have some inkling of what it could be but basically, I'm in the dark about it.

Guess I've yakked and yakked enough and it's time for me to close! You mentioned Rockefeller in your last letter and I agree with you that he's certainly no liberal but simply trying to disguise himself as one—a poor attempt! He is certainly a major leader of world imperialism, hav-ing control over key industries, with the help of his family ties. I think his main interest in taking the VP position is to assume control directly over economic matters. It shows the type of crisis capitalism is today that he must come into national politics in this manner.

I think he's uninterested in the job as Pres. *per se* but more concerned with directing the economy into a more favorable position for himself. And his peers. Ford is not in the driver's seat, a mere smokescreen, a kind of window dressing, to direct attention to this man for all people, a refreshing change from Nixon and concession to Congress to boot.

The resignation of Nixon is the most drastic and earth shaking of developments in the history of the US since 1929. I can no way overstate the profundity of this move. No way! The press, govt, and professional sellers of state (intellectual prostitutes) have banded together to try and make his move seem like just another day in the life of usual everyday occurrences, and that all is well. But, it is far from well, for the political/eco. system of this country. It takes a lot of power to unseat a US president without an election and it calls for a lot of instability for an unelected officer of state (unelected to Pres, unelected to VP) and even his home district is now Democrat, to stand as Pres.

It is a hard, desperate sell being made on us! Congress goes for him because he's conceded to recognize Congress' new power and relations in Govt. and the bourgeoisie like him because he's lean and loyal enough to take the back seat and play the figurehead (be the figurehead!).

The power that amassed against Nixon was a groundswell of resentment from the people that was but irresistibly followed by Congress in an attempt to prevent a truer, more open outbreak of the people.

The coming days and months promise to be more demanding, exciting, and trying for us as the very own dynamics of the system pursue itself to a resolution. I want to be with you all, my adrenaline and pulse rates are high and I'm anxious to contribute to these definitive days for the Twenty-First century.

Love ya,
Ernest

EPILOGUE

WEEKS FOLLOWING MY PAROLE INTERVIEW — after even more weeks of efforts throughout the summer by family and community members who were demanding my release on parole, and even after receiving word that State Rep. George "Mickey" Leland, out of Houston's Fifth Ward, had issued a press release notifying the prison authorities that he'd use the Governor's official plane to come to the prison to secure my release — I finally received my inexplicably delayed release date from the Parole Board. It was December 21, three years and two weeks after my capture in Cincinnati.

It is a long-held custom among prisoners to keep one's actual release date to oneself. If anyone inquires, the wisest, most "unjinxable" response is to say that you haven't received your parole notification yet. On the day before I was transported to Huntsville to be freed, I divided all my books between my celly and those who I felt would fully welcome them. To Huntsville, I carried only the clothes on my back, a box of letters accumulated over the years, valued legal documents, and notes. Clothes I wore when captured over three years before in Cincinnati, and stored in the Walls Unit, were given back to me. I was handed an envelope that held a hundred dollars, the state's obligatory sum issued to all those exiting the walls.

Waiting for me outside on that cool but bright, sunny afternoon were Sandra Thompson — my dear comrade, sister, and love — and

Charles Hill, my new brother-in-law, married now to my sister Jackie. Sandra was looking so good! I held her tightly in my arms and whispered, "Thank God, thank God!" into each ear as I took in her kisses from ear to ear. Charles stood patiently by, smiling broadly while tugging on a fancy-looking pipe. I reached out hugging Charles and Sandra together, exhaled a shout of relief and joy to the heavens, thanking them again and again for coming to get me. It felt so unreal to see the walls behind me now—me, standing on the outside of the towers with those armed, Confederate-uniformed sentinels now turning their backs from us and facing the inside perimeters slowly.

Arriving in Dallas—seeing and finally being able to hug, to fully embrace, my mother, sisters, cousins, aunts, and uncles over the next few days—was an exhilarating feeling and precious reminder of how life can transform so quickly, so profoundly in a matter of three years. My mother served up my favorite dishes on my first evening home. In those first few days I was able to unite with former Dallas SNCC comrades Black Ed Harris, Marilyn Clark, Kwesi and Genie Williams, Mike Morris (aka Babuki), Charlie Paul Henderson (aka Kaleef Hasan), Ruth Jefferson, Jackie Harris, "Mickey" McGuire, and the newly joined and veteran fellow travelers Taft Baker, Bill Stoner (aka Sababu), Karioki, Mary Greene, Al Lipscomb, Charlie Young, and others.

I felt hopeful about possibilities working together, but I also felt tremendous pressure to be "that guy," to pick up from where things once stood in Dallas. Felicia had remarried and lived with Ohene and her new expanding family in Michigan. In Dallas, the Black Panthers, the SCLC, the Green Berets, the Bois D'Arc Patriots, and the Third Eye were actively engaged in wide-ranging, highly connected concerns and projects: police reform, electoral politics, Black consciousness economic development, and more. I began to feel a stronger need for emphasizing and organizing sustainable, vitally needed community organizations prioritizing mentorship and youth development—empowering youths to become our future leaders. Others, including the sinister white power structure as well as old allies and acquaintances seemed to expect the "Old Ernie" to continue, repeat the actions of the '60s.

State Rep. Eddie Bernice Johnson invited me to take on a staff position in her office, as a legislative aide, and when I accepted, she called a press conference to announce it. My primary duties were to become a link to the community, responsible for responding to needs and requests from her constituents and to spend about one week out of each month in Austin during the legislative sessions attending to political liaison duties. I served at that post for about a year and was discharged when Johnson learned I had become campaign manager for Al Lipscomb, who was running for city council. She disapproved of his highly controversial political stances and felt I was somehow dragging her name, her office into the political fray. Al, on the other hand, was a much-beloved grassroots community activist who needed organizational capacity building. I was excited to lend a hand. Leaving her office was a jump into the briar patch, like a fish being tossed back into the waters.

I did not know very clearly then what my next steps would be. My bubbling embryonic vision was a longing for a brighter future—one that possessed a deeply rooted faith in the upcoming generations, our next waves, very capable of lifting the movement for liberation to a higher ground. It contained notions for building community institutions and generating a fledgling reservoir of youth leaders, who would be skilled in the art of listening, internalizing, and regenerating their heritage, learning from our mistakes and misfortunes, all the while carrying the hopes and dreams of our people forward. Such new leaders would be the peaceful warriors we'd prayed for, less encumbered by egocentric compulsions, anchored by a burning heart for the collective will being synthesized and expressed foremost.

I had little conception of how the course might run, the costs or sacrifices to be made. Yet, all in all, I felt willingly compelled to risk going there.

I was ready.

ACKNOWLEDGMENTS

I would like to extend my thanks to:

The exquisite creative production team: Anyika McMillan-Herod, Chris Herod, Kijana Martin, Michael Tate, and Jennifer Gunn, for their constant care and support. They initiated the entire book process, instilled confidence in me to dare to try, and never gave up on me, this project.

The final launch dream team composed of dear souls, family members, and longtime friends, as well as a newly entrusted one, all with an unyielding faith in me, my mumblings, the book's calling, and its possibilities for contributing to a rekindling of the movement for justice, self-determination, and a beloved community. They are Christina Hahn, Dafina Toussainte McMillan, Jackie McMillan-Hill, Kathy McMillan, Marilyn Clark, Marcus Kaunda Wesson, and Reymundo Morales. They effectively guided, tugged, pulled, and encouraged me through to the finish line.

The publishing team: visionary publisher Will Evans and his outstanding staff at Deep Vellum—Sara Balabanlilar, Kirkby Gann Tittle, Serena Reiser, Riley Rennhack, Walker Rutter-Bowman, and Linda Stack-Nelson—and editor extraordinaire Zac Crain. Much gratitude for your ever-persistent faith and diligence throughout this meandering endeavor.